super grains & seeds

super grains & seeds

wholesome ways
to enjoy super foods
every day

RYLAND PETERS & SMALL
LONDON • NEW YORK

Amy Ruth Finegold

Photography by Clare Winfield

Senior Designer Sonya Nathoo
Commissioning Editor Stephanie Milner
Production Manager Gary Hayes
Art Director Leslie Harrington
Editorial Director Julia Charles

Prop Stylist Joanna Harris
Food Stylist Rosie Reynolds
Indexer Sandra Shotter

First published in 2014 by Ryland Peters & Small
20–21 Jockey's Fields, London WC1R 4BW
and
519 Broadway, 5th Floor, New York NY 10012
www.rylandpeters.com

10 9 8 7 6 5 4 3 2 1

Notes
• All spoon measurements are level unless
otherwise specified.
• All eggs are medium (UK) or large (US)
unless otherwise specified.
• Ovens should be preheated to the specified
temperatures. All ovens work slightly differently.
We recommend using an oven thermometer
and suggest you consult the maker's handbook
for any special instructions, particularly if you
are cooking in a fan-assisted/convection oven,
as you will need to adjust temperatures according
to manufacturer's instructions.

Printed and bound in China

contents

foreword

This book isn't just a journey of travel and cuisine, it's a journey of my own health. Having struggled with digestion and related health problems for over 20 years, I have learnt that digestive health is at the core of our well-being. I am not a doctor, but I am a patient. A doctor could suggest what to do, but it was my body that had the answer. The field of gastroenterology offered plenty of abstract diagnoses, but had no real answers, so as a teenager I took matters into my own hands. Trial, error and motivation were the tools I used to discover the path to my own health.

I went through my early adult life as a childhood educator, with a hidden passion for healthy cooking. I was accumulating a vast amount of nutritional knowledge that so many people were just beginning to explore. There are dozens of digestive ailments and diseases that can be significantly improved with the right diet. My diet is high in the foods of this book and also mostly dairy-, sugar-, and gluten-free. With help from doctors, taking influence from Eastern medicine and common sense, I taught myself how to eat focusing on mind, body and balance. I believe we should eat foods that come from the earth. Foods that are natural and ironically 'ancient'. Quinoa was my first passion. Then came amaranth, millet and rice. The flours from these grains captured my interest and I became an expert on gluten-free flours. I made baking mixes solely for my own use, so I could eat and make muffins to share with friends. After my son, Jake, was born, selling my gluten-free baking mixes was a natural progression. The need was there and the health market continues to explode with superfoods and ancient grains.

For the past 8 years, I travelled extensively, spending most of my time in London, New York and California. As such, there are many different ingredients and cuisines represented in this book. What excited me most in my travels was how different parts of the world use grains in various ways. Indian cuisine takes flour from chickpeas and uses it to make pancakes. Head over to Turkey and bulgur is the staple in their diet. I had fun drawing from my travels and incorporating them into this book. From Moroccan chicken tagines to California's roasted kombucha squash, I've dressed these grains up for everyone to enjoy.

Wholegrains and seeds are no longer a trend – they are here to stay. The staple of many ancient cultures, cafés in all major cities now serve wholegrain salads and seeded bread. Some of these grains and seeds are even called 'superfoods' because they are very high in nutrients, protein and fibre. Even better is that they have the nutrition and taste to stand alone as a meal. I feel part of this health food revolution and the recipes in this book are a true reflection of the meals I eat. I love teaching people what I know. I've had to suffer a great deal to be in this position of helping people. It's part of who I am, it's the journey that was handed to me. I feel honoured to have achieved this. If even one recipe has inspired you or given you the knowledge to make a change for your own health or of someone that you love, then this book is already a success.

understanding grains & seeds

This book focuses on whole grains and seeds, which form the main part of my diet, along with fruits, vegetables, healthy fats and protein. I chose the grains and seeds that feature because of their health benefits, accessibility and versatility. I've divided the grains into those that contain gluten and those that are gluten-free. A gluten-free substitute is noted alongside any recipe in this book that uses a grain containing gluten for those who are avoiding gluten altogether.

cooking grains

Cooking grains can seem intimidating but they are more forgiving than we think. To simplify, there are two general ways to cook grains. One is the 'absorption' method where grains are cooked slowly in a specific amount of liquid until tender. I use this for quinoa, millet, amaranth and bulgur.

The other way is the 'pasta' method, where grains are cooked in an abundance of water and then drained once cooked. I recommend this for firmer grains, including barley, buckwheat, farro and wheatberries.

For the more experienced chef, there is also the 'toast absorption' method – a variation of the 'absorption' method – where you toast the grains before the liquid is added to increase the amount of flavour in a dish.

tips for storage

I recommend storing seeds and grains (rinsing if not pre-rinsed) in sterilized airtight containers

in the cupboard. It's best to store flour in the refrigerator to prolong its shelf life. Grains stay fresh for up to 3 days in the refrigerator once cooked but they can also be frozen. Some grains freeze better than others and most gluten-free grains are best eaten fresh. Any gluten-free grains used in soups are also suitable to freeze.

grains that contain gluten

Gluten is a protein commonly found in wheat and wheat related species. Many wholegrains do contain this protein but if you do not have a gluten issue, then these grains are wonderful additions to your diet.

Barley
Barley is a high-fibre, nutty-flavoured grain that is most commonly used in soups. It is sold in many forms, depending on how much of the outer covering is removed. I recommend hull-less barley so the bran layer is still intact, with the most outer layer removed. This retains the nutrition from the bran layer but it needs a longer cooking time than other barleys as well as soaking the night before. Pearl barley is most commonly available, but it has been stripped of most of the bran layer so it's not considered a wholegrain. Besides soup, barley is a great side dish to meat.

Bulgur
Bulgur, a common grain in the Middle East, is cracked wheat, which is quick to cook. It is traditionally used in tabbouleh but can be made into any cold grain salad. Nutritionally, it is high in fibre and low in calories so it's a great grain for weight loss.

Farro
These are whole-wheat kernels that are common in Tuscan cooking. Sweet, chewy, and nutty, they are great in salads and soups. Nutritionally it is high in fibre, magnesium, vitamins A, E and B.

Freekeh
Freekah is a form of wheat but one of high nutritional value. It is harvested when the wheat is young and has a smoky flavour. Because of its high fibre and protein content, it is commonly used in salads and side dishes.

Kamut
Kamut is also a type of wheat that is high in protein and minerals. It has a higher percentage of lipids – naturally occurring fats and oils – than other grains, making it a good energy source. Larger than other grains, kamut holds its own in dishes like pilafs.

Spelt
Spelt is another nutrient powerhouse in the wheat family. It has a high water solubility so nutrients are easily absorbed and it becomes easier to digest. It is also high in fibre. Those with a mild gluten sensitivity often tolerate the gluten in spelt. Spelt flour is great to bake with for those who can tolerate gluten.

Wheatberries
Wheatberries are actual wheat kernels with the husks removed, so they still have the germ and endosperm intact. This makes them high in nutrients like protein, fibre and iron. They take a long time to cook and require soaking overnight but they make the base of a great salad or can be enjoyed as a warm pilaf.

gluten-free grains

Although this is not a gluten-free book, I have marked substitute gluten-free grains for recipes that feature grains that contain gluten. In recent studies, up to 1 in 100 people are now allergic to the protein – a condition called coeliac disease. As a result a growing number of people are avoiding gluten in their diets. Whether you are a coeliac, gluten sensitive, or have someone you cook for that is, knowing which grains are gluten-free is very important. Many of these grains like quinoa, millet and amaranth are related to plant and grass species, rather than wheat. These gluten-free grains can be used in their flour form as well, which is convenient for the gluten-free baker.

Amaranth

Amaranth was cultivated by Aztecs and Incas, and has a similar nutritional value to quinoa. Like quinoa, it is also a grass. High in protein, calcium, potassium, magnesium and folic acid, it's a grain that is definitely worth trying. A small ancient grain, amaranth retains a little texture once cooked. It is tasty hot, as a pilaf, or as a porridge, but you can also take the cooked grain and add it to pancake batter to give it a nutritional and tasty punch. I find that the flour from amaranth is best for cookie recipes.

Buckwheat

Unlike its name, buckwheat is completely wheat-free and comes from the seed of a plant related to rhubarb. It contains all of the essential amino acids, calcium, potassium, iron, and zinc. Two very different cultures have traditionally used this grain in very different ways. Buckwheat takes the form of soba noodles in Asian cuisine but in Ashkenazi Jewish culture, *kasha varnishkes* is a traditional dish of bowtie pasta mixed with buckwheat. Buckwheat is available as both grain and flour, with the flour commonly used to make pancake batter. They are dense, darker and have a stronger flavour than traditional white pancakes.

Millet

Millet used to be considered food for the birds but it has now earned its place at the table. It's best eaten hot and is a great grain substitution for couscous. Millet flour is now commonly sold in health food markets and is a perfect substitute flour to use as the base of bread, since it is hearty

and has a mild taste. Millet is high in nutrients such as magnesium and manganese.

Quinoa

This is ultimately my favourite grain. It is perhaps the most versatile grain as you can have it sweet, savoury, cold, hot, and it tastes good leftover too. The most common colours are white and red, although it is also available in black or purple. Quinoa is a complete food, containing all essential amino acids. It's high in protein, iron, potassium and phosphorous and is easily digestible. Technically not a grain, quinoa is related to the grass species.

Rice: Brown, Black & Red

White rice is not considered a wholegrain because it is stripped of its outer layer, which removes all of the nutrients. Fortunately, there are many varieties of wholegrain rice that are widely accessible. They come in different colours like black and red, which I love because it's always fun to add a splash of colour to the dinner plate.

Rice: Wholegrain

Wholegrain rice is rich in fibre, antioxidants, and vitamin B6. It is proven to improve weight loss when used as a substitute to white rice, reducing body fat and lowering body mass index (BMI). I prefer eating these grains served warm, flavoured with coconut.

Rice: Wild

Wild rice is actually an edible grass. Nutritionally, it has a much better profile than any other rice as it is rich in antioxidants, fibre, minerals and protein. Wild rice has a pleasant nutty taste, which goes really well in salads with soft roasted vegetables or fruit, and is delicious hot and cold.

Teff

Teff is the smallest of the gluten-free grains, but it is not small in nutritional value. Higher in calcium and vitamin C than any other grain, teff is best used as a flour in baked goods. It comes from Ethiopia, where they use it to bake bread called *injera*.

seeds

Seeds are a nutritionally wondrous food. For their size, they contain an incredible amount of fibre, nutrients and healthy fats. Most are available in raw seed form as well as oil and spread forms. The oil from seeds can replace regular vegetable or olive oil in cooking and contains more healthy omega fatty acids too. Spread forms make great alternatives to butter. Many vegans use seeds as a staple part of their diet to make up for the vitamins that they miss out on from not eating meat or dairy. The seeds I use in the recipes within this book represent those I eat most but there are new varieties of seeds on sale in whole foor stores all the time, so keep an eye out for the next super seed.

Chia seeds

Chia seeds come from the edible plant Salvia hispanica. They have a higher omega 3 content than flaxseeds and can be consumed milled in the same way. The seed itself has the unique ability to soak up liquid, making a gel that can be the base of desserts and drinks. Chia can expand to more than 8 times their weight in water. They also have a high fibre and nutrient content.

Flaxseeds

Both flax- and chia seeds have a great omega 3–6 oil ratio profile. This is highly regarded because the fat is mostly from a plant source. Flaxseeds are best eaten milled since they can be added to almost anything. They are known for their high fibre and nutrient content. Flaxseed is also available in oil form.

Hemp seeds

Hemp seeds are a top nutritional food. They have the same prized omega 3–6 oil ratio as flax- and chia seeds and contain all of the essential amino acids. Like flax- and chia seeds, they have a high percentage of fibre as well as protein. Hemp has an earthy taste which can be bitter. I could eat hemp seeds raw, but they are best mixed into something already delicious to please picky palates.

Pumpkin seeds

Pumpkin seeds, also known as *pepitas*, are high in antioxidants, omega 3 and zinc. They make a great snack and perfect roasted on salads. In spread form they add a rich, nutty flavour so why not spread a paste of pumpkin seeds on your bread instead of butter?

Sesame seeds

These tiny seeds are high in calcium, magnesium and vitamin E. They possess fibres called lignans, which fight bad cholesterol. Sesame seed oil contains healthy fats and is used extensively in Asian cuisine because its strong taste pairs well with other Asian flavours.

Sunflower seeds

Sunflower seeds are the perfect snack. Loaded with healthy fat and nutrients, they satisfy hunger, aid digestion and keeping you going until your next meal. I buy them roasted and take them when I travel to eat as a snack. They are the go-to seed for sprinkling on salads and are often found at salad bars.

other healthy ingredients

'Superfood' is a catchy word. It is used to describe foods that are exceptional in nutritional value. You can argue that many of the wholegrains and seeds in this book are superfoods but there are a few other foods worth noting that I use regularly in this book and at home. They aren't in the grain or seed category but they are very versatile to cook and bake with and are a healthy addition to any diet. They are nutritional powerhouses, high in antioxidents, rich in fibre and packed full of potassium – super!

Acai

This berry is a small, dark, round purple fruit. It has a very concentrated amount of antioxidants and also contains oleic acid – a healthy fat – and amino acids. This truly is a wonder fruit that is also sold in powder form and in frozen blocks. The frozen blocks have a dense, rich, thick consistency when blended so make delicious smoothies and breakfast bowls.

Almond flour

Almonds are high in monounsaturated fats and protein but low in carbohydrates. With a low glycaemic index (GI), almond flour is a healthy food that's also easy to use because of its natural fat content.

Coconut oil

Coconut oil contains medium-chain fatty acids that are very good for you because of how the body metabolizes them. It has a delicious flavour, is a topical moisturiser and is great for your hair and skin too! It is delicious in baked goods and because refined coconut oil has a higher cooking point than other oils it is more versatile for baking at very hot temperatures.

breakfast

I'm a believer in breakfast. It is the most important meal of the day. From oat cereal and pancakes to muffins and smoothies, these recipes will energize and fuel your body when it needs it most.

hearty oat groat cereal with acai purée

oat cereal
190 g/1 cup rolled
  porridge oats/oat groats
720 ml/3 cups water
2 tablespoons almond milk
maple syrup, to taste

acai purée
100 g/1 sheet frozen
  acai purée
1 small banana, frozen
180 ml/¾ cup almond milk
1 teaspoon maple syrup

fresh fruit, to garnish

serves 2

Don't get me wrong, quick-cook porridge is healthy and I'm always thrilled when my son eats it for breakfast (with added flaxseeds of course), but oat groats are higher up on the unprocessed grain chain, adding more fibre. Acai is a superfood of the berry world and is sold as a frozen purée or in powder form in health food stores. It is easy to incorporate in a super-charged cereal and this dish pops up on menus in healthy cafés all over California as a breakfast bowl.

If using oat groats you will need to soak them in water in a medium saucepan or pot the night before. In the morning, bring the soaked oats to a boil, then cook on a low boil with the lid off for 30 minutes. The water will evaporate to create a mushy, rice-like consistency. If using porridge oats, follow cooking instruction on packet. Scoop the mix into two bowls. Add the almond milk and maple syrup into each and stir.

Put all of the ingredients for the acai purée in a food processor and blend until you have a thick and silky consistency. Pour acai purée on top of the oats, covering them completely, and garnish with fresh fruit. Raspberries, blackberries and cherries work particularly well. Serve immediately.

amaranth porridge

720 ml/3 cups water
190 g/1 cup dry amaranth
3 tablespoons almond milk
40 g/¼ cup raisins (soaked
  in warm water for
  3 minutes)
1 banana, sliced
1 teaspoon cinnamon
1 tablespoon maple syrup,
  or to taste

serves 2

Amaranth is a nice alternative to your traditional porridge. It's silky like Cream of Wheat or Ready brek but with a slight al dente texture. Amaranth is gluten-free and a powerhouse of nutrients.

Bring the water to the boil in a medium saucepan or pot. Add the amaranth, stir, cover, and simmer with the lid on for about 30 minutes. Turn off the heat, stir in the almond milk and make sure to stir out any clumps. Add in the raisins, banana, cinnamon and maple syrup.

You could also add flaxseeds, hemp seeds or bran for an extra boost of nutrients.

Serve immediately in a bowl.

buckwheat & flaxseed pancakes

50 g/⅓ cup potato starch
½ teaspoon bicarbonate
  of soda/baking soda
1½ teaspoons baking
  powder
70 g/½ cup buckwheat
  flour
60 g/½ cup brown rice
  flour
3 tablespoons milled
  flaxseeds
½ teaspoon sea salt
1 teaspoon cinnamon
480 ml/2 cups almond
  milk
2 eggs (see Note)
1 teaspoon vanilla extract
vegetable oil, for shallow
  frying
maple syrup, to taste
a handful of blueberries,
  to serve (optional)

serves 2–4

As a child, Saturday mornings meant pancakes with maple syrup. My mother used to make an annual drive to the best sugar farm in New England to stock up on the highest quality maple syrup for the whole year and I still remember those jugs of liquid gold lined up in our pantry. Like many other recipes in this book, I've upped the nutrition factor by taking out white wheat flour as the base and adding wholegrain flours and flaxseeds. But don't skimp on the syrup – that's the best bit!

Sift the potato starch, bicarbonate of soda/baking soda and baking powder into a mixing bowl. Add in the remaining dry ingredients and set aside. In another bowl, combine the almond milk, eggs and vanilla extract. Add the wet into the dry ingredients gradually and whisk to a thick batter.

Heat the oil in a frying pan/skillet over a medium–high heat. Drop the batter from a spoon into the pan to form round circles. Cook until small bubbles form on the top of each pancake. Flip and cook for a further 3 minutes or until golden brown in colour.

Serve immediately, stacked on a plate and drizzled with maple syrup. Blueberries make a tasty addition, if desired, and are a powerful antioxidant.

Note: If you prefer not to use eggs you could use egg replacer or make a flax-egg mix by combining 2 tablespoons of ground flaxseed with 6 tablespoons of water.

coconut breakfast cookies

½ teaspoon bicarbonate
   of soda/baking soda
½ teaspoon xanthan gum
1 teaspoon cinnamon
65 g/½ cup coconut flour
   or kamut flour
15 g/⅛ cup flaxseeds
2 eggs (see Note)
1 teaspoon vanilla extract
60 ml/¼ cup almond milk
60 ml/¼ cup melted
   coconut butter
28 g/⅓ cup gluten-free
   oats
2 tablespoons shredded
   coconut
2 tablespoons maple syrup
50 g/⅓ cup dried figs
170 g/¾ cup chopped
   pineapple in its juice
   from a can

*a baking sheet lined with
baking parchment*

*makes approximately
18 cookies*

*One of my best friends craved these cookies while she had to follow
a strict gluten-, dairy- and soy-free diet, so I used to churn out a lot
of them. Coconut flour is low-GI flour. It is unique to work with
because it soaks up a lot of liquid. You can substitute ripe mashed
banana for the fruit purée, it will still be delicious!*

Preheat the oven to 180ºC (350ºF) Gas 4.

Sift the bicarbonate of soda/baking soda, xanthan gum and cinnamon
into a mixing bowl.

Roughly purée the pineapple in its juice in a food processor and add to
the mix. Add in the remaining ingredients one at a time and stir until
the fruit has a good coating of batter. Cover and chill in the refrigerator
for around 20 minutes.

Once chilled, use a tablespoon to measure equally sized balls of cookie
dough and space each out on the prepared baking sheet. Press each ball
down with your finger to flatten the mix slightly and make an imprint.

Bake for 12–15 minutes until golden and serve.

*Note: If you prefer not to use eggs you could use egg replacer or make a flax-
egg mix by combining 2 tablespoons of ground flaxseed with 6 tablespoons
of water.*

pineapple bran muffins

125 g/¾ cup dried fruit
(I used raisins and figs
for this)

125 g/½ cup low-fat
yogurt

60 ml/¼ cup vegetable oil

1 egg (see Note)

35 g/¼ cup potato starch

½ teaspoon bicarbonate
of soda/baking soda

½ teaspoon baking powder

½ teaspoon xanthan gum

30 g/¼ cup brown rice
flour

30 g/¼ cup teff flour

2 tablespoons milled
flaxseeds

105 g/¾ cup oat bran

70 g/⅓ cup sugar or
sweetener

a handful of chopped
pineapple

a muffin pan lined with
parchment paper or paper
cases

makes approximately
10 muffins

A friend challenged me to make her favourite coffee shop muffin with my mixes. I added an extra step by plumping up and blending dried fruit but if you need a short cut, just use store bought organic baby food. It gives a great consistency and flavour! The final word on these muffins: 'I'd pay £3 for just one'. Success!

Preheat the oven to 180ºC (350ºF) Gas 4.

Put the dried fruit in a mixing bowl and cover it with very hot but not boiling water. Leave to soak for 10 minutes, drain, and discard the water. Then purée the fruit in a food processor. If you don't have time to plump the fruit you can substitute 125 g/½ cup of store bought fruit flavoured baby food.

Mix the dried fruit purée with the rest of the wet ingredients. Sift in the starch, bicarbonate of soda/baking soda, baking powder and xanthan gum. Then add in the remaining dry ingredients and beat until fully mixed. Lastly, fold in the chopped pineapple.

Spoon the muffin mixture into the prepared muffin pan. Bake for 20 minutes until cooked through and golden brown on top.

These can be eaten hot or cold but are really delicious served warm, straight from the oven.

Note: If you prefer not to use eggs you could use egg replacer or make a flax-egg mix by combining 1 tablespoon of ground flaxseed with 3 tablespoons of water.

dairy-free blueberry heaven yogurt berry muffins

70 g/½ cup potato starch

1 teaspoon bicarbonate of soda/baking soda

1 teaspoon baking powder

1 teaspoon xanthan gum

60 g/½ cup brown rice flour

60 g/½ cup teff flour

3 tablespoons milled flaxseeds

125 g/½ cup coconut yogurt

2 eggs (see Note)

70 ml/⅓ cup vegetable oil

70 ml/⅓ cup maple syrup or agave syrup

180 ml/½ cup apple or pear purée (available online)

1 teaspoon vanilla extract

a large handful of blueberries

a muffin pan lined with baking parchment or paper cases

makes approximately 10 muffins

These are hands down the best gluten-free muffins I have ever eaten. You can make a sliceable loaf cake if preferred – simply bake the mixture in a parchment paper lined loaf pan for 35 minutes.

Preheat the oven to 180ºC (350ºF) Gas 4.

Sift the potato starch, bicarbonate of soda/baking soda, baking powder and xanthan gum into a mixing bowl. Add in the remaining dry ingredients then beat the wet ingredients into the mix one at a time, before folding in the blueberries.

You can also substitute the apple or pear purée for store bought fruit flavoured baby food.

Spoon the muffin mixture into the prepared muffin pan. Bake for 17 minutes or until cooked through and golden brown on top.

Serve immediately or store in an airtight container for a lunchtime treat.

Note: If you'd rather not use eggs you could use egg replacer or make a flax-egg mix by combining 2 tablespoons of ground flaxseed with 6 tablespoons of water.

sweet spinach & hemp smoothie

50 g/2 handfuls baby
   spinach
90 g/½ cup fresh or canned
   pineapple
240 ml/1 cup coconut milk
60 g/½ cup ice
½ frozen banana
2 tablespoons milled hemp
   seeds or 1 tablespoon
   hemp powder

serves 1

This is a great way to get your greens along with hemp, a superfood seed. Hemp is another complete food, containing all the essential amino acids. I like to camouflage hemp with a little tropical fruit so its nutty undertones appeal to all.

Start by preparing the fresh ingredients. Wash and destalk the spinach then skin, core and dice the pineapple or drain if using canned pineapple.

Purée all ingredients in a food processor until you have a smooth, liquid consistency. Serve in a large glass.

papaya chia smoothie

2 tablespoons chia gel
   (see method)
215 g/1 heaping cup
   chopped frozen papaya
240 ml/1 cup almond milk
175 ml/¾ cup coconut
   water
1 teaspoon fresh lime juice
1 teaspoon agave syrup

serves 1

Papaya is my favourite morning fruit and it's conveniently loaded with digestive enzymes. It emulsifies into a creamy consistency when blended into a drink which is perfect for smoothies and shakes. Smoothies are a brilliant way to mix in superfoods like chia seeds, which are loaded with essential omega fatty acids, fibre and protein. Chia seeds soak up a lot of liquid so it's best to make a 'gel' the night before. Using frozen fruit instead of ice cubes is a great trick for smoothies and a clever way to preserve fruit.

Start by preparing the chia gel. A few hours or the night before, put one tablespoon of chia seeds in a bowl with 5 tablespoons of water and just mix with a fork. The chia seeds will expand to a thick, gloopy consistency. You can store any left over gel in the refrigerator for up to 3 days.

Purée all ingredients in a food processor until the frozen fruit has dissolved. Serve in a large glass.

chocolate almond butter smoothie

240 ml/1 cup almond milk
1½ tablespoons cacao
    powder
1 teaspoon maca powder
2 tablespoons almond
    butter
90 g/¾ cup ice
½ banana
2 teaspoons agave syrup

serves 1

Cacao powder is raw and unprocessed, containing minerals and antioxidants. In its purest form, we now know that chocolate is good for you! I make this when I feel like having a milkshake for breakfast. Almond butter is great to have in the morning since it is a satisfying and healthy fat. I add maca powder too, which comes from a root packed with minerals and B vitamins. You can omit the maca, or add any other health powder of choice like lucuma or acai, both superfood powders that are available from health food stores.

The beauty of this recipe is its simplicity as well as its chocolate-y nature. Simply purée all the ingredients in a food processor until smooth.

Serve in a large glass.

variation

If you prefer not to use banana you could substitute frozen pear here. The taste is just as good and pear acts as a natural sweetener which blends beautifully with the chocolate for a super-sweet morning treat.

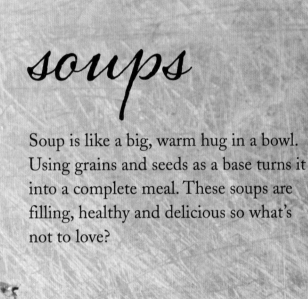

soups

Soup is like a big, warm hug in a bowl. Using grains and seeds as a base turns it into a complete meal. These soups are filling, healthy and delicious so what's not to love?

2 tablespoons vegetable oil
1 large onion, finely
    chopped
1 teaspoon cumin seeds
1 teaspoon ground
    coriander
1 teaspoon chilli powder
2 garlic cloves, finely
    chopped
200 g/7 oz canned
    chopped tomatoes
950 ml/4 cups water
425 g/15 oz black beans
2 teaspoons freshly
    squeezed lime juice
1 tablespoon chopped
    coriander/cilantro
sea salt and freshly ground
    black pepper, to taste

super chia garnish
1 tablespoon chia seeds
4 tablespoons crème fraîche
1 teaspoon freshly
    squeezed lime juice
a pinch of sea salt

serves 4

black bean soup with super chia garnish

There is nothing wrong with using canned beans to create a super, fresh tasting, easy dinner. Hiding a super seed in the salsa adds an extra health punch too!

For the super chia garnish, toss all the ingredients in a bowl and chill in the refrigerator while you make the soup so the chia seeds expand.

Heat the oil in a frying pan/skillet and fry the onion, cumin seeds, coriander and chilli powders over a medium heat for 5–8 minutes until the onions are translucent. Add the garlic and fry for a minute longer. Then add the chopped tomatoes, water and black beans and stir. Reduce the temperature, cover and cook for 15 minutes. Set aside to cool.

Once cooled, purée the soup in a food processor. Adjust the seasoning if required. Return to the heat and warm through. Serve in bowls, with a squeeze of lime juice (about a teaspoon each) and garnish with fresh coriander/cilantro and a dollop of the garnish.

gorgeous green detox soup

1 tablespoon butter

1 tablespoon olive oil

1 medium onion, chopped

2 garlic cloves, chopped

500 g/18 oz (about 4 medium) courgettes/zucchini

240 ml/1 cup water

480 ml/2 cups vegetable stock

100 g/3½ oz fresh spinach

1 tablespoon sea salt

1 teaspoon freshly ground black pepper

a handful of chopped mint, plus extra to garnish

2 tablespoons milled hemp seeds

4 tablespoons crème fraîche, to garnish

serves 4–6

Whatever ails me, this is the recipe that I turn to. Whether it's my stomach or throat, I can easily throw this together when I am feeling under the weather. Some people are cured by chicken soup, I'm cured by cooked greens. It's also the first thing I would recommend to jumpstart a diet.

Heat the butter and oil in a large saucepan or pot over a high heat. Fry the onion in the saucepan for 10 minutes or until translucent. Add the garlic then reduce the temperature and add the courgettes/zucchini, water and stock to the pan. Slowly bring to the boil, then cover and simmer for 10 minutes.

At the end, add the spinach, season, and cook for a further 5 minutes. Set aside to cool slightly.

Once cooled, purée the soup with the mint and hemp seeds in a food processor. Return to the heat and warm through. Serve in bowls and garnish with a dollop of crème fraîche and a few small mint leaves.

cauliflower soup with roasted pumpkin seeds

30 g/¼ cup pumpkin seeds
2 teaspoons Himalayan
   salt
1 medium onion, chopped
1 tablespoon olive oil
3 garlic cloves, chopped
1 large head cauliflower
   (cut into small florets)
1 tablespoon butter
480 ml/2 cups water
700 ml/3 cups vegetable
   stock
120 ml/½ cup
   unsweetened light
   coconut milk

serves 4–6

I love making soups that taste creamy without the cream. The trick is to use a generous amount of the featured vegetable and using a good quality food processor to purée it to the right consistency. Another trick is to use a little coconut milk, which can fool any dairy lover. I usually end up snacking on the roasted pumpkin seeds before they make it into the soup as a garnish!

Prepare the roasted pumpkin seeds in advance. Preheat the oven to 150ºC (300ºF) Gas 2. Spread the seeds evenly on an oiled baking sheet and sprinkle half of the salt on top. Roast for about 30 minutes, checking on them after 15 minutes to make sure they are toasting evenly.

In a large saucepan or pot, fry the onion in olive oil over medium–high heat for about 5 minutes or until translucent. Lower the heat slightly, add the garlic, and fry for another minute or so. Remove from the heat.

In a separate frying pan/skillet, fry half of the cauliflower in the butter. Cook until the cauliflower is toasted. Transfer the cooked cauliflower into a bowl and set aside. Repeat the cooking process with the rest of the cauliflower – this prevents overcrowding in the pan to make sure all the ingredients are cooked evenly.

Once your cauliflower is cooked add it all to the pan of fried onion and garlic with the water, remaining salt and vegetable stock. Bring to the boil, then cover and simmer for 30 minutes. Remove from the heat and stir in the coconut milk.

Purée the soup in a food processor. Return to the heat and warm through. To serve, ladle the soup into bowls and garnish with the pumpkin seeds.

summer melon soup with tamarind

1 teaspoon chopped fresh
ginger
1 tablespoon grapeseed oil
3 tablespoons chopped
spring onion/scallion,
plus extra to garnish
1 star anise, plus extra
crushed to garnish
3 teaspoons tamarind
paste
160 g/1 cup chopped
melon/cantaloupe flesh
160 g/1 cup watermelon
1 medium cucumber,
peeled
sea salt and freshly ground
black pepper, to taste

serves 2

Before I was old enough to appreciate the marriage of dissimilar tastes, I never understood why my grandfather put salt on melon. This soup makes me think of him since tamarind is a South Asian fruit that is both sweet and sour. I know he would have loved my take on this melon soup, except knowing him, he'd probably still add more salt!

In a small saucepan or pot, fry the ginger in grapeseed oil with the spring onion/scallion and the star anise for 3 minutes. Reduce the heat, add the tamarind paste and cook for another minute.

Remove the star anise and set aside to cool.

Purée the cantaloupe, watermelon and cucumber together in a food processor. Then add the cooled tamarind sauce and purée again.

Adjust the seasoning with salt and pepper and serve cold in bowls. Garnish with crushed star anise and a handful of chopped spring onion/scallion.

avocado soup

4 avocados
freshly squeezed juice
of 2 lemons
1 medium cucumber,
peeled
1 teaspoon sea salt
480 ml/2 cups vegetable
stock
1 teaspoon ground
coriander
2 tablespoons milled hemp
seeds
a sprig of dill, to garnish

serves 4

Avocados are a wondrous food. They contain healthy fats that nourish the body inside and out and are a surprising source of fibre. This is a simple way to make a refreshing and satisfying soup.

Place all the ingredients in a food processor and purée until smooth. Pour into a mixing bowl or jug, cover and chill in the refrigerator.

Stir the hemp seeds through the soup then serve cool with a garnish of fresh dill.

roasted asparagus & farro soup

In London, I always looked forward to June when asparagus was at the peak of its season. I spent every Sunday at the farmers' market, come rain or shine. It would be full of gorgeous bunches of asparagus and fresh soups. Roasting asparagus gives this soup a depth of flavour that makes it extra special. For a gluten-free variation, replace the farro with brown rice or quinoa.

185 g/1 cup dried farro
750 ml/3 cups water
900 g/2 lb asparagus
2 small shallots, chopped
2 tablespoons olive oil
1 teaspoon Himalayan salt
1 teaspoon freshly ground
   black pepper
2 garlic cloves, crushed
1 litre/4 cups low sodium

vegetable stock
1 teaspoon allspice
a handful of fresh flat-leaf
   parsley
the grated zest of 1 unwaxed
   lemon

*2 large baking sheets lined with
   baking parchment*

serves 4

Preheat the oven to 190°C (375°F) Gas 5.

Rinse the farro under cold, running water in a sieve/strainer. Put the farro and water in a large saucepan or pot on a high heat and bring to the boil. Reduce the heat, cover and simmer for 15 minutes, then drain and set aside.

Rinse and trim the asparagus, discarding the bottom ends of the asparagus. Lay on one of the prepared baking sheets with the shallots. Drizzle with oil, season well with salt, pepper and add the garlic. Roast for 20 minutes, turning once.

Purée the cooked asparagus in two batches together with 500 ml/2 cups of vegetable stock in the first batch and the remainder in the second. Transfer the liquid to a saucepan or pot.

Bring the soup to a simmer over high heat and stir in the allspice. Add a little extra water to reach the desired consistency if needed. Add the drained farro and season to taste.

Serve in bowls and garnish with fresh parsley and lemon zest.

lentil & squash soup

1 large onion, finely
 chopped
2 teaspoons sea salt
2 tablespoons vegetable oil
2 garlic cloves, chopped
1 teaspoon chopped fresh
 ginger
2 teaspoons ground cumin
1 teaspoon chilli powder
1 teaspoon turmeric
2 teaspoons ground
 coriander
350 g/2 cups red lentils
1.4 litres/6 cups water
500 ml/2 cups vegetable
 stock
500 g/3 cups chopped
 butternut squash
2 tablespoons flaxseed oil
a handful of fresh
 coriander/cilantro,
 to garnish

serves 8–10

Red lentils take the prize as my favourite pulse. Why? They are quick to cook, tasty, and easy to digest. Red lentils and squash marry well with Indian spices. Spices like turmeric, ginger and coriander are great for digestive health. I always make a big batch of this soup because it freezes really well.

In a large saucepan or pot, fry the onions and salt in vegetable oil until the onions are soft. Add the garlic, ginger and spices and fry for about 1 minute.

Put the lentils in the bottom of the pan and coat them with the spice mixture. Add the water, vegetable stock and squash and bring to the boil. Reduce the heat, cover and simmer for about 20–30 minutes. Set aside to cool slightly.

Once cooled, purée the soup in a food processor, add the flaxseed oil and adjust the seasoning as required. Return to the heat and warm through.

Serve in bowls and garnish with fresh coriander/cilantro. The soup can be stored in the freezer for up to 3 months.

cold tomato soup with flaxseeds

1 medium carrot, peeled
and chopped
1 onion, chopped
2 tablespoons olive oil
1 garlic clove, chopped
500 ml/2 cups vegetable
stock
800 g/1 lb 12 oz fresh
tomatoes, deseeded and
chopped
1 teaspoon sea salt
1 teaspoon freshly ground
black pepper
20 g/½ cup chopped fresh
basil, plus a few leaves
to garnish
2 teaspoons tomato
purée/paste
2 tablespoons finely milled
flaxseeds
freshly squeezed juice
of 1 lemon

serves 4

We can't always get our hands on perfect tomatoes, so this is a great refreshing summer soup regardless of the tomato season. Although, if you happen to have access to amazing tomatoes, go ahead and chop them up and leave the can in the pantry.

In a large saucepan or pot fry the carrot and onion in the oil over a medium– high heat until translucent. Add the garlic and stir for 1 minute. Then add the vegetable stock, tomatoes, salt, pepper, basil and tomato purée. Bring to the boil, reduce the heat, cover and cook for 20 minutes. Set aside to cool slightly.

Once cooled, purée the soup in a food processor, adjust the seasoning as required and chill. When you are ready to serve, stir in the flaxseeds and squeeze some lemon juice onto each portion. Garnish with fresh basil and extra pepper, if desired.

quinoa soup with red beans and kale

175 g/1 cup dried red
 kidney beans
1 onion, chopped
1 green (bell) pepper,
 chopped
2 celery stalks, chopped
2 tablespoons olive oil
2 garlic cloves, finely
 chopped
300 ml/1¼ cups vegetable
 stock
750 ml/3 cups water
160 g/¾ cup quinoa
2 teaspoons dried oregano
a pinch of cayenne pepper
2 teaspoons paprika
100 g/1 large bunch kale
sea salt and freshly ground
 black pepper, to taste

serves 4-6

This is a great take on a Southern Cajun soup, using the superfoods kale and quinoa. I prefer kale to be wilted as I find it easier to digest. Taking the step to purée some of the beans and stock is necessary to get the perfect consistency but on a busy school night, I always substitute kidney beans from a jar.

Put the dry red kidney beans in a bowl and soak in water overnight. When you are ready to make the soup, drain and set aside.

In a large saucepan or pot, heat the onion, green pepper and celery in oil over a medium heat. Cook for about 3 minutes or until the onion is translucent. Then add the garlic, stir, and cook for another minute. Put the drained red kidney beans into the pan with the vegetable stock and water. Bring the liquid to a boil then reduce the heat, cover and simmer until the beans are tender. This usually takes around 50 minutes.

Remove 500 ml/2 cups of the stock and 2 teaspoons of the beans and purée in a food processor. Then return the thickened purée to the pan.

Now add the quinoa, herbs and spices. Return to the boil, then reduce the heat, cover and simmer for 15 minutes. Meanwhile, prepare the kale.

Wash the kale in cold water. Then trim the stems and rough chop the leaves. After the quinoa has been cooking for 15 minutes, add the kale. Cover and continue to cook for another 8 minutes, until the quinoa is fully cooked.

Add salt and pepper to taste and serve immediately.

chicken soup with black forbidden rice

chicken broth
1 chicken (cut into
8 pieces, bones and
skin left on)
4 carrots
1 onion, peeled and
quartered
1 parsnip
2 celery stalks
1 bay leaf
4 sprigs of fresh dill
a handful of chopped fresh
flat-leaf parsley

130 g/1 cup cooked black
rice (see method)
2 carrots, chopped
1 celery stalk, chopped
a handful of chopped fresh
flat-leaf parsley and dill,
to garnish

serves 4

Black rice has its origin in China and I highly recommend it as a new grain to try. It has a pleasantly mild, nutty flavour and its colour makes for striking presentation. As a Jewish woman, there really is only the traditional way to make good chicken soup so I recommend doing this a day ahead. In honour of my favourite children's book author, Maurice Sendak, 'cooking once, cooking twice, cooking chicken soup with rice!'

Put all of the chicken broth ingredients in a large saucepan or pot on a medium–high heat. Cover with water and bring to the boil. Reduce the heat, cover and simmer for 1 hour.

Remove the white breast meat so that it doesn't overcook and set aside in the refrigerator. Return the bones to the pan and simmer for another hour. Strain the broth and chill in the refrigerator overnight.
(I usually eat the overcooked veggie mush, but you can discard it.)

The next day, cut or shred the chicken into bite-size pieces. Then cook the black rice according to packet instruction or using the ratio of 200 g/ 1 cup of rice to 420 ml/1¾ cups of water.

Put the rice and water in a medium saucepan or pot and bring to the boil. Reduce to a low heat, cover and simmer for 30 minutes. Remove from the heat, fluff with a fork, then put the lid back on and set aside for 5 minutes.

Skim the fat off the top of the broth and pour into a large saucepan or pot. Add in the carrots, celery and black rice. Cook for about 5 minutes or until the vegetables are tender, then add the shredded chicken and cook until heated through.

Serve immediately and garnish with chopped parsley and dill.

salads & snacks

You wouldn't necessarily think to feature ancient grains as the main part of a salad or as the essential ingredients in a cracker. Here, they take centre stage and deservedly so.

avocado, rocket & grapefruit salad with sunflower seeds

2 medium ripe avocados
2 pink grapefruits
100 g/4 cups rocket/
arugula

vinaigrette
1 teaspoon clear honey
3 tablespoons champagne
vinegar
4 tablespoons flaxseed oil
3 tablespoons sunflower
seeds
sea salt and freshly ground
black pepper, to taste

serves 4

This is a recipe my grandmother used to entertain with. She had special crescent moon shaped dishes, just for this starter. It's elegant, simple and classic. I've added some sunflower seeds and flaxseed oil to boost the omega 3 content. And any size or shape plate will work fine!

Prepare the avocados. Using a sharp knife, cut an avocado in half, turning it as you do to cut around the stone. Twist the two halves to separate. Remove the stone and peel the two halves. Repeat with the second avocado then slice the flesh and set aside.

Now prepare the grapefruit. Peel the fruit whole then break into individual segments. Using a sharp knife, carefully score the straight edge of each segment then peel the membrane from the flesh. Repeat until you have released all the deliciously juicy segments.

For the vinaigrette, whisk the honey, champagne vinegar and flaxseed oil together in a mixing bowl, adding the sunflower seeds at the last minute so as not to damage them. Season to taste.

Place a layer of rocket/arugula on each plate. Arrange the grapefruit and avocado on top, with alternating slices of grapefruit and avocado in concentric semi-circles. You needn't arrange the fruit in this way if you're in a hurry but it looks great when entertaining. Lightly drizzle a line of vinaigrette horizontally across the half-moons of alternating grapefruit and avocado. Enjoy immediately.

quinoa salad with spring vegetables & herbs in a citrus dressing

315 g/1½ cups white
quinoa
360 ml/1½ cups vegetable
stock
300 ml/1¼ cups water
1 avocado
40 g/¼ cup segmented and
chopped clementines
45 g/⅓ cup thinly sliced
radishes
70 g/⅔ cup watercress,
plus extra to serve
45 g/¼ cup pomegranate
seeds
40 g/¼ cup pine nuts
8 g/⅛ cup basil leaves
15 g/¼ cup chopped
flat-leaf parsley

citrus dressing:
6 tablespoons flaxseed oil
2 tablespoons freshly
squeezed lemon juice
freshly squeezed juice
of 2 clementines
1 teaspoon clear honey
1 teaspoon Dijon mustard
sea salt and freshly ground
black pepper, to taste

serves 4–6

*If you want to convert a friend to the wonders of quinoa,
I recommend serving this for lunch. There is nothing as enticing
as a gorgeous quinoa salad, which looks almost too pretty to eat.
My number 1 grain, showcased as it should be.*

Put the dry quinoa in a large saucepan or pot with the vegetable stock
and water over a medium–high heat. Bring to the boil then lower the
heat, cover and simmer for 20 minutes. Remove from the heat, fluff with
a fork, cover once more and let it sit for another 5 minutes. Remove the
lid and set aside to cool.

Prepare the remaining salad ingredients. Chop the avocado and
clementines into bite-size pieces and finely slice the radishes. Mix them
all together in a separate bowl with the watercress, pomegranate seeds,
and pine nuts. Gently roll and finely chop the basil and flat-leaf parsley
then add to the mix.

For the dressing, whisk together the flaxseed oil, lemon and clementine
juices, honey and Dijon mustard. Season with salt and pepper to taste.

Mix the quinoa with the bowl of vegetables and seeds and drizzle the
dressing on top.

Serve on individual plates with extra watercress and dressing to the side,
if desired.

shaved broccoli & buckwheat salad with dukkah topping

240 ml/1 cup vegetable stock

185 g/1 cup buckwheat groats

240 ml/1 cup water

4 broccoli stalks

15 g/⅛ cup chopped hazelnuts

dressing:

300 g/1 cup plain yogurt

freshly squeezed juice of 2 lemons

½ teaspoon sea salt

½ teaspoon cumin powder

a bunch of freshly chopped coriander/ cilantro

dukkah topping:

2 teaspoons cumin seeds

2 teaspoons coriander seeds

1 teaspoon fennel seeds

100 g/¾ cup roasted hazelnuts, chopped*

100 g/¾ cup roasted sunflower seeds*

1 teaspoon sea salt

*see page 36 for instructions on home roasting

serves 4–6

When you pay for vegetables in weight, one becomes a lot more conscious of waste. When I chop up broccoli florets for my son's dinner, I usually use the stalks for soup. This salad uses the forgotten broccoli stems that can be quite attractive shaved into strips. Buckwheat, one of our great supergrains, is nice for this but wheatberries would be just as good for those who are not on a strict gluten-free diet. Dukkah is a special addition to any salad. It is made up of crushed seeds, nuts and spices that are tasty and great for digestion. That's a win-win for me! I like to keep a big batch in my fridge to sprinkle on roasted vegetables.

In a large saucepan or pot, put the vegetable stock, water and buckwheat groats over a medium–high heat. Bring to a boil, then turn down the heat and simmer for 15 minutes with the lid half on, stirring once half way through. Be careful not to overcook the groats. Drain and rinse with cold water then set aside in a bowl to cool.

Peel and shave the broccoli stalks into ribbons using a vegetable peeler or mandolin then add to a large saucepan or pot of boiling water. Cook for 3 minutes then shock the broccoli to suspend the cooking by submerging it in a bowl of iced water. Drain, cool and mix with the hazelnuts and reserved buckwheat.

For the dressing, whisk all the ingredients together and store in the refrigerator until you are ready to serve.

For the dukkah topping, use a pestle and mortar to grind the cumin, coriander and fennel seeds by hand. Blend the hazelnuts and sunflower seeds in a food processor to a roughly chopped consistency. Mix in a bowl with the crushed spices then set aside. This should yield about 200 g/1½ cups of dukkah.

To serve, spoon the broccoli and buckwheat mix onto individual plates, drizzle over the dressing and cover each serving with a tablespoon of dukkah topping.

wild rice with artichoke, peaches & pine nuts

190 g/1 cup wild rice

1 litre/4 cups water

400 g/1½ cups artichokes soaked in water (rinsed and drained)

a bunch of freshly chopped coriander/cilantro

30 g/¼ cup pine nuts

60 g/½ cup chopped peaches

dressing

3 tablespoons walnut oil

2 tablespoons freshly squeezed lemon juice

½ teaspoon sea salt

½ teaspoon freshly ground black pepper

serves 2–4

Wild rice is actually an edible grass, which has a slightly nutty and chewy flavour. It form the base of a great grain salad – just add your favourite veggies and a simple vinaigrette. Since it's a hearty grain, I've paired it with soft artichokes, which are high in antioxidants.

Bring the water to a boil in a large saucepan or pot over a high heat. Add the wild rice, reduce the heat, cover and simmer for 45 minutes. Drain any excess water and set aside.

For the dressing, whisk together the walnut oil, lemon juice, salt and pepper in a large bowl.

Then once the rice has cooled a bit but is still slightly warm, mix in the dressing with the artichokes, half of the coriander/cilantro, pine nuts and peaches.

Serve with an extra garnish of coriander/cilantro.

shredded carrot & courgette salad with sesame miso sauce

2 carrots, grated
3 courgettes/zucchini, grated
30 g/¼ cup sesame seeds
150 g/1 cup firm tofu, chopped (optional)

miso dressing:
2 tablespoons miso paste
1 tablespoon rice wine vinegar
1 tablespoon sesame oil
2 tablespoons flaxseed oil
1 teaspoon finely sliced fresh ginger
2 teaspoons clear honey

serves 2-4

Vegetables take on a new personality when they are prepared differently. Japanese cuisine can turn a simple radish into a piece of art. The simple act of shredding veggies and mixing in a delicious dressing is a tasty and beautiful way to treat our senses.

Put the carrots, courgettes/zucchini, sesame seeds and tofu in a bowl. The tofu is optional but I recommend eating this as a meal and not as a side because tofu goes so well with the miso dressing.

For the dressing, whisk all of the ingredients together to an emulsion. Pour over the mixed salad and serve.

The salad can be prepared in advance and stored in the refrigerator for up to 2 days.

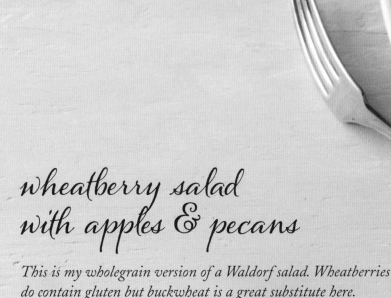

wheatberry salad with apples & pecans

This is my wholegrain version of a Waldorf salad. Wheatberries do contain gluten but buckwheat is a great substitute here.

200 g/1 cup wheatberries
1 green apple, chopped
65 g/½ cup pecans
100 g/2 cups mixed salad
  leaves

dressing
50g/scant ¼ cup
  mayonnaise
50g/scant ¼ cup low-fat
  plain yogurt
3 tablespoons freshly
  squeezed lemon juice
½ teaspoon sea salt
½ teaspoon freshly ground
  black pepper

serves 2-4

Put the wheatberries in a medium-sized saucepan or pot and cover completely with water by 2½ cm/1 inch. Bring to the boil over a high heat then reduce the temperature and simmer uncovered for about 50 minutes. Remove from the heat, drain and set aside.

In a large bowl, make the dressing by whisking together the mayonnaise, yogurt, lemon juice, salt and pepper. Add the apples, pecans and wheatberries and using salad tongs or a large spoon, gently fold all of the ingredients together.

Plate the salad leaves first, then add the wheatberry mix on top. Serve immediately as the apple will discolour.

spelt & spinach salad with pear & prosciutto

200 g/1 cup spelt berries
460 ml/2 cups water
a handful of fresh thyme
100 g/4 cups baby spinach,
  chopped
2 pears, sliced
12 slices prosciutto
  or Parma ham
sea salt and freshly ground
  black pepper, to taste

dressing
3½ tablespoons balsamic
  vinegar
6 tablespoons olive oil

serves 4

Spelt is an ancient grain that is a relative of wheat. It isn't technically gluten-free so those with coeliac intolerances should substitute buckwheat in this recipe. However, many with wheat sensitivities are able to eat spelt berries because they are unrefined. Pears and prosciutto are great vehicles for an excellent balsamic vinegar. The best ones come from Modena in Italy. On my travels, I was lucky enough to visit a family-owned producer of this liquid gold. It's so good, you can eat it right from the spoon.

Soak the spelt berries in water overnight. Drain and put in a saucepan or pot. Pour in the water (making sure it's enough to cover the spelt berries). Bring to the boil over a high heat then reduce the temperature, cover and simmer for 45 minutes. Remove the lid and drain if there is any excess water. Put in a separate bowl and leave to cool.

While the spelt berries are cooling, make the dressing by whisking 2 tablespoons of the balsamic vinegar together with the olive oil.

Dress the spelt berries with the balsamic vinaigrette and sprinkle in the fresh thyme leaves. Mix in the spinach. Season with salt and pepper.

To build the salad, scatter the spelt, spinach and thyme mixture on a serving plate. Layer the sliced pears and prosciutto on top.

Drizzle the extra 1½ tablespoons of balsamic vinegar over the pears and prosciutto and serve immediately.

red quinoa chicken & mushroom salad with harissa vinaigrette

200 g/1 cup red quinoa
240 ml/1 cup vegetable
    stock
220 ml/1 scant cup water
300 g/4½ cups sliced
    mushrooms
2 shallots
2 tablespoons vegetable oil
120 g/½ cup pulled
    pre-cooked chicken
a large bunch of freshly
    chopped flat-leaf parsley,
    to garnish

harissa vinaigrette:
3 teaspoons harissa paste
3 tablespoons flaxseed oil
3 tablespoons freshly
    squeezed lemon juice
1 tablespoon red wine
    vinegar

serves 2

One of my closest friends is a professionally-trained chef. She assembles the most amazing salads and dressings, with textures and flavours that always impress. Harissa, a North African hot red spice blend, is a flavour that she introduced me to. The combination of harissa and fresh parsley is so delicious. You can prepare this salad in advance for when you know you will have leftover chicken, ready to assemble just before serving.

Put the quinoa in a large saucepan or pot with the vegetable stock and water over a medium–high heat. Bring to the boil then lower the heat, cover and simmer for 20 minutes. Remove from the heat, fluff with a fork, cover once more and let it sit for another 5 minutes. Remove the lid and set aside to cool.

While the quinoa cooks, fry the mushrooms with the shallots in vegetable oil in a frying pan/skillet for 8–10 minutes or until the mushrooms are cooked. Remove from the heat and leave to cool.

For the vinaigrette, whisk the harissa paste, flaxseed oil, lemon juice and red wine vinegar together.

When you are ready to serve, add the mushrooms and chicken to the quinoa. Toss to combine and pour over the dressing. Garnish with the fresh parsley.

410 g/2½ cups white beans
freshly squeezed juice
   of 1 lemon
freshly squeezed juice
   of 1 clementine
1 peeled garlic clove
50 g/1 cup spinach
3 tablespoons flaxseed oil
Himalayan salt and freshly
   ground black pepper,
   to taste

crostini
1 wholegrain baguette
   or 6 wholegrain
   gluten-free rolls
120 ml/½ cup
   garlic-infused olive oil

serves 4

white bean & spinach dip with wholegrain crostini

Using seed oils in dips is a great way to load up on your omega 3s while whipping up an elegant side dish. This is a beautiful, light green dip that looks great garnished with fresh herbs. Serve with carrot sticks, white jícama, or crostini, as here.

For the crostini, preheat the oven to 180ºC (350ºF) Gas 4.

Slice the baguette or rolls into 1-cm/½-inch slices. Brush both sides of the sliced baguette or rolls with garlic-infused olive oil then arrange the pieces on a baking sheet. Season with salt and pepper.

Bake the slices in the preheated oven for 20 minutes, turning once so both sides cook evenly and brown. Transfer the crostini to a wire rack to cool then serve with the white bean dip.

For the dip, blend all of the ingredients together in a food processor and serve. It's as easy as that! I like to add the spinach at the end and leave it coarsely chopped so I can see little dark green flecks.

beetroot herb dip with seeded amaranth crackers

2 garlic bulbs, unpeeled
4 beetroot/beets, tops and
  bottoms trimmed
3 tablespoons flaxseed oil
1½ teaspoons ground
  sumac
1 teaspoon cumin seeds
freshly squeezed juice
  of 1 lemon
1 teaspoon sea salt
freshly ground black
  pepper, to taste
a handful of fresh coriander/
  cilantro, to garnish

amaranth crackers
45 g/⅓ cup amaranth flour
40 g/⅓ cup milled flaxseeds
40 g/¼ cup sunflower seeds
1 teaspoon sea salt
¼ teaspoon onion powder
  or ½ small chopped onion
20 g/⅛ cup pumpkin seeds
2 tablespoons milled hemp
  seeds
1 tablespoon melted
  coconut oil, plus extra
  for greasing
60 ml/¼ cup water

*2 baking sheets lined with
  aluminium foil*

serves 4

You eat with your eyes with this dip! Beetroot is as nutritious as it is colourful. Sumac is a great North African and Middle Eastern spice, also used in the spice blend Za'atar. Seeds make nutty and delicious crackers! You can make a cracker purely from seeds, but I like to add a bit of amaranth flour so it has a little more substance to it while still retaining a crispy texture.

For the dip, preheat the oven to 180ºC (350ºF) Gas 4.

Wrap the garlic in foil and put on one of the prepared baking sheets. Wrap the beetroot/ beets in a separate sheet of foil and put on the same baking sheet. Roast the beetroot/beets and garlic for 30 minutes, then remove the garlic and set aside. Roast the beetroot/ beets for a further 30 minutes or until tender, then allow to cool.

Peel the garlic and the beetroot/beets (this is the messy part so feel free to wear gloves!) and blend them in a food processor with the flaxseed oil, sumac, cumin seeds, lemon juice, salt and pepper. Add more flaxseed oil as required to reach the desired consistency.

For the crackers, preheat the oven to 150ºC (300ºF) Gas 2. Grease the second prepared baking sheet with a thin layer of coconut oil.

Pulse all of the dry ingredients in a food processor – you can leave the seeds in a roughly chopped state, if you prefer more texture. Then add the coconut oil and water and blend again until all the ingredients come together into a dough. Roll the dough thinly onto the prepared baking sheet and bake for 45–50 minutes. Set aside to cool, then break into pieces. Store in an airtight container until ready to serve.

Transfer the dip to a serving bowl, garnish with fresh coriander/cilantro and serve with the crackers.

flax-speckled hoummus with kale crisps

It's so easy to make your own hoummus and it's a great way to control the kind of oil you consume. This recipe is a double dose of flax because it uses both flaxseeds and flaxseed oil, so it's a great source of omega 3s. Kale, one of the best green superfoods, is delicious as a crisp for this!

400 g/3 cups cooked chickpeas
2 tablespoons tahini paste
freshly squeezed juice of 2 large
    lemons
2 tablespoons water
2 crushed garlic cloves
1 teaspoon ground cumin
1 tablespoon flaxseed oil
1 tablespoon milled flaxseeds
sea salt and freshly ground black
    pepper, to taste

kale chips

1 medium head of curly kale
2 tablespoons olive oil
1 tablespoon Parmesan cheese
    or nutritional yeast flakes if you
    are dairy-free
1 teaspoon onion powder or 2 small
    chopped onions
½ teaspoon Himalayan salt

serves 4

For the hoummus, blend all of the ingredients in a food processor and serve!

For the kale crisps, preheat the oven to 95ºC (200ºF) Gas ¼.

Wash and dry the kale. Mix the oil, Parmesan/nutritional yeast flakes, onion powder/chopped onion and salt in a bowl. Add the kale leaves to the bowl and coat with the oil mixture. Put the kale leaves on a baking sheet and cook for 45 minutes. Keep an eye on them so as not to burn the edges.

Cool and serve with the hoummus or store in an airtight container for up to 3 days.

aubergine dip with almond chia crackers

800 g/2 large
   aubergines/eggplants
2 tablespoons grapeseed
   oil
½ teaspoon Himalayan salt
2 garlic cloves
2 tablespoons freshly
   squeezed lemon juice
3 tablespoons flaxseed oil
sea salt and freshly ground
   black pepper, to taste

almond chia crackers
60 g/½ cup almond flour
30 g/¼ cup coconut flour
30 g/¼ cup ground chia
   seeds
¾ teaspoon sea salt
½ teaspoon onion powder
   or 1 chopped small
   onion
60 ml/¼ cup olive oil
60 ml/¼ cup water

*makes 12 crackers
and serves 2*

*In London, I used to live around the corner from 3 different
Lebanese restaurants. Hoummus and baba ganoush were staples
when ordering in. Baba ganoush traditionally has tahini paste
in it but I've left it out to create more of a purist aubergine dip.*

Preheat the oven to 200ºC (400ºF) Gas 6.

Cut the aubergine/eggplant in half and pierce the skin and flesh several
times. Put on a baking sheet, drizzle with grapeseed oil, sprinkle with
salt and bake skin side up for 35–40 minutes or until the flesh is tender.
Remove from the oven and cool in a bowl of iced water. This will make it
easier to peel away the skins.

Peel and discard the skins and add the flesh to the garlic, lemon juice and
flaxseed oil in a food processor. Blend, season with salt and pepper and
store in the refrigerator until you are ready to serve.

For the crackers, preheat the oven to 180ºC (350ºF) Gas 4.

Add all of the dry ingredients to a mixing bowl. Then add the oil and
water and mix to form a ball with your hands. Chill in the refrigerator in
clingfilm/plastic wrap for 20 minutes. Then roll out as thinly as possible
on a rectangular non-stick baking sheet. Bake for 15 minutes then
remove from the oven, leave to cool and cut into pieces.

Transfer the dip to a serving bowl and serve with these super-chia
crackers or pita bread.

main dishes

All of a sudden the dinner table has got a lot
more exciting! See how you can use millet as
a stuffing, incorporate bulgur into a seafood
pilaf, and use seeds as a crust for any fish.

quinoa crusted quiche with mushroom & courgette

125 g/⅔ cup quinoa flour

40 g/⅓ cup potato starch

35 g/¼ cup ground flaxseeds

½ teaspoon sea salt

¼ teaspoon freshly ground black pepper

110 g/8 tablespoons unsalted butter, diced

6 tablespoons iced water

filling

1 onion, chopped

2 tablespoons vegetable oil

110 g/1½ cups sliced mushrooms

1 medium courgette/ zucchini, chopped

100 g/4 cups spinach

4 eggs plus 3 egg whites

a handful of fresh dill

1 tablespoon quinoa flour

1½ teaspoon potato starch

3 tablespoons goat's cheese (optional)

an 8-inch tart pan/pie plate, greased

serves 6

Vegetables that you've forgotten about in the fridge can be easily turned into an elegant Sunday brunch. Just whip up eggs and sauté whatever veggies you have to hand, and you'll wonder why you don't do it more often. The trick is the crust. I love teaching people how to make a quinoa crust. Quinoa's natural nutty flavour makes a lovely crust for a pie or quiche.

In a food processor, mix the dry ingredients. Then pulse the cold butter in, add the water and pulse further. The mix will come together so after a minute, scoop it out and form a ball in your hand.

Wrap the dough in clingfilm/plastic wrap and refrigerate for 30 minutes. Once chilled, press it into the prepared tart pan and poke holes in the base with a fork

Preheat the oven to 180ºC (350ºF) Gas 4.

Bake the pastry case in the preheated oven for 20 minutes then remove from the oven once crisp. Do not turn off the oven but set the case aside at room temperature.

Meanwhile, make the filling, fry the onion with 1 tablespoon of vegetable oil until translucent. Add the mushrooms and courgette/zucchini and another tablespoon of oil to the pan and continue to fry. Once the vegetables are cooked, drain any excess liquid from the mixture and set aside. In the same pan, wilt the spinach adding water if required. Drain any excess liquid from spinach then put the cooked spinach, with the mushroom and courgette/zucchini mixture and leave to cool.

In a separate bowl, whisk together the eggs, egg whites, flour, potato starch and goat's cheese. The cheese gives a creamy texture but you can leave it out if preferred. Add the cooled vegetable mixture then pour into the pastry crust. Bake in the still-hot oven for a further 35 minutes until the top is slightly golden. Slice and serve hot or cold.

roasted kobucha squash with avocado yogurt hemp dressing

1 kobucha squash
a drizzle of olive oil
a pinch of sea salt
a pinch of freshly ground
    black pepper

dressing
1 avocado (see preparation
    method on page 52)
3 tablespoons plain
    full-fat yogurt
2 teaspoons of hemp
    seeds, plus extra to serve
freshly squeezed juice
    of ½ a small lemon
1 tablespoon chopped
    fresh dill, to garnish

serves 2

Kobucha squash is the best kept secret of the squash world. It is sweeter and creamier than its relative, butternut squash. The best part is that the skins are tender, so you can devour the whole thing (I've even made them into fries!) It's also a great vehicle to showcase any sweet or savoury topping. When I'm in California, this is one way I like to use up avocados.

Preheat the oven to 180ºC (350ºF) Gas 4 then line a baking sheet with aluminium foil.

Cut the squash in half and spoon out the seeds. Put the squash, either in halves or slices, on the baking sheet and drizzle with olive oil. Season with salt and pepper. Roast in the preheated oven for 30–45 minutes, until tender. Remove from the oven and set aside at room temperature.

For the dressing, first prepare the avocado following the instructions on page 52. Then mash the avocado flesh with the remaining ingredients with a fork until fully mixed – you needn't use a food processor. Pour the dressing over the squash and sprinkle with extra milled hemp seeds and chopped dill.

spiced chickpea pancakes with tzatziki

1 small onion, chopped
6 tablespoons vegetable oil
1 tablespoon butter
200 g/2 cups chickpea
    flour
1 teaspoon salt
¼ teaspoon turmeric
¼ teaspoon ground
    cayenne pepper
415 ml/1¾ cups water
2 tablespoons freshly
    squeezed lemon juice
85 g/½ cup chopped
    tomatoes
1 teaspoon cumin seeds

tzatziki:
2 tablespoons chopped
    fresh dill
1 small cucumber
500 g/2 cups low-fat
    Greek yogurt
2 tablespoons flaxseed oil
1 garlic clove, crushed
1 teaspoon Himalayan salt

*makes approximately
10 pancakes*

Another reason why I fell in love with Indian cuisine is that they use different wholesome grains like rice and beans as the base of a dish instead of wheat. It was so easy to follow a gluten-free diet in India! Here is a pancake made from chickpea (or gram) flour.

Fry the onion in a small frying pan/skillet with a tablespoon of vegetable oil and butter until translucent, then set aside.

Sift the chickpea flour, salt, turmeric, and cayenne pepper in a mixing bowl. Slowly, stir in half of the water and lemon juice, whisking until there are no lumps. Then slowly add the rest of the water. Add the tomatoes, reserved onion and cumin seeds. Leave the batter to rest.

For the tzatziki, chop the dill and cucumber then mix all the ingredients together in a large bowl. Taste and adjust the salt seasoning.

When ready to cook the pancakes, put 2 teaspoons of vegetable oil in a large non-stick frying pan/skillet over medium–high heat. Ladle a large spoonful of batter into the pan and tip to each side to coat the base of the pan like you would a crêpe. Drizzle another teaspoon of vegetable oil over the top and cook for about 3 minutes. Flip the pancake and cook for another 1–2 minutes.

Plate the warm pancakes with tzatziki on the side and enjoy!

polenta tart with goat's cheese & tomatoes

1 litre/4 cups water
170 g/1 cup polenta
1 tablespoon butter
  (optional)
1 teaspoon sea salt
1 teaspoon freshly ground
  black pepper

topping
300 g/1 cup cherry
  tomatoes
1½ teaspoons sea salt
1½ teaspoons freshly
  ground black pepper
1 tablespoon olive oil
150 g/6 oz goat's cheese
a handful of fresh basil
  leaves, to garnish

*a rectangular baking sheet,
  greased*

serves 4–6

Sometimes I forget that corn has its place as a grain. There are rougher cuts of corn as a grain, known as polenta, with some of the bran layer in tact which count as a wholegrain.

For the topping, cut the tomatoes in half and mix together with the salt, pepper and olive oil. Set aside.

Preheat the oven to 180ºC (350ºF) Gas 4.

Bring the water to the boil in a large saucepan or pot, then slowly pour in the polenta while whisking. Whisk for five minutes until fully combined. Reduce the heat, then cover and cook for 15 minutes, stirring vigorously every 5 minutes. Remove the lid, then add a tablespoon of butter, if desired, and the salt and pepper. Stir together then pour onto the prepared baking sheet and bake in the preheated oven for 20 minutes.

Remove from the oven and allow to cool completely before cutting into square portions of equal size.

Put some of the tomato topping on each square and sprinkle with a little goat's cheese. Garnish with torn fresh basil and season with a little extra salt and pepper, then serve immediately.

buckwheat noodles with pak choi, cashews & tamari sauce

340 g/12 oz buckwheat
  noodles
1 onion
1 tablespoon finely
  chopped fresh ginger
1 tablespoon grapeseed
  oil
200 g/1 large head pak
  choi/bok choy
50 g/½ cup roasted
  cashew nuts (see Note)

tamari sauce

1 tablespoon soy sauce
  (check for gluten-free)
2 teaspoons sesame oil
¼ teaspoon finely
  chopped ginger
2 teaspoons flaxseed oil
2 teaspoons clear honey
1 tablespoon freshly
  squeezed lemon juice
1 tablespoon white
  sesame seeds

serves 4

This is a great go-to Asian dish. Buckwheat flour is often used in noodle dishes. Some buckwheat noodles do have wheat in them so check the package if you want them wheat-free! This recipe uses the same tamari sauce as the Asian slaw on page 100, proving its versatility.

Prepare the tamari sauce in advance. Whisk all of the ingredients together in a large bowl until combined.

Cook the noodles in salted water in a large saucepan or pot over a medium heat for 10-12 minutes, or according to the packet instructions.

While the noodles are cooking, chop the onion, ginger and pak choi/bok choy. In a large frying pan/skillet, fry the onion and ginger in the grapeseed oil until the onion is translucent. Add the chopped pak choi/bok choy, until wilted.

Drain the noodles, then mix together with the fried vegetables in the reserved bowl of tamari sauce. Toss with chopped roasted cashew nuts and serve.

Note: If you can't find pre-roasted cashews you can roast them yourself by scattering them on an ungreased baking sheet and cooking in a preheated oven at 180ºC (350ºF) Gas 4 for 10 minutes, or until golden.

millet stuffed squash with caramelized onions, kale & raisins

80 g/½ cup raisins
2 acorn squash
2 tablespoons olive oil
a pinch of sea salt
95 g/½ cup dry millet
2 tablespoons butter
300 ml/1¼ cup low-sodium
   vegetable stock
1 large onion, chopped
1 tablespoon butter
1 tablespoon olive oil
1 tablespoon clear honey
1 teaspoon paprika
½ teaspoon chilli powder
100 g/½ head of kale
sea salt and freshly ground
   black pepper, to taste

*a baking sheet lined with
   aluminium foil*

serves 2

Millet is an underused nutrient and dense grain. It is best eaten right after it is cooked as a substitute for couscous because it tends to dry out once it cools. Since millet is a hearty grain, it pairs well here with the soft sweet flesh of an acorn squash.

Preheat the oven to 180°C (350°F) Gas 4. Soak the raising in water for 20 minutes then drain and set aside.

To prepare the squash, cut them in half and scoop out the seeds inside. You should have a decent size cavity that will eventually hold the millet stuffing. Put the halves on the prepared baking sheet. Drizzle with olive oil and salt and bake in the preheated oven, flat side down, for 40 minutes, or until the flesh is tender.

While the squash is cooking, toast the millet with the 2 tablespoons of butter in a large saucepan or pot over a medium heat for 3–5 minutes, until you can smell a toasty aroma. Add the vegetable stock and bring to the boil. Reduce the heat, cover and simmer for 20 minutes. Then fluff with a fork, turn the heat off and let it sit, covered, for another 5 minutes.

While the millet cooks, fry the onions, butter and olive oil in a large frying pan/skillet until translucent. Add the honey and cook until the onions caramelize. Then add the paprika, chilli powder and drained raisins. Stir for 3 minutes, then put the mixture in a bowl and set aside.

In the same pan, steam the kale by putting 240 ml/1 cup water in the pan. Add the kale and cover with a lid to steam for 8 minutes, stirring after 4 minutes, until the leaves wilt. Remove the kale with a slotted spoon and add it to the fried onion mixture.

Add the millet to the kale and fried onion mixture and stir so that the millet is coated in flavour. Adjust the seasoning with salt and pepper.

Once the acorn squash are baked, turn them over and generously scoop a large spoonful of the millet filling into each cavity. Serve hot.

quinoa burgers with portobello mushrooms

3 tablespoons olive oil

1 onion, finely chopped

2 garlic cloves, crushed

75 g/½ cup black beans

120 g/1 cup cooked quinoa
(see Note)

100 g/½ cup sweet potato,
flesh scooped out

1 carrot, shredded

½ teaspoon ground cumin

½ teaspoon ground
coriander

2 tablespoons parsley,
chopped

15 g/⅛ cup gluten-free
breadcrumbs

5 portobello mushrooms

a pinch each of sea salt
and freshly ground
black pepper

to serve

1 avocado, sliced (see
method on page 52)

1 large tomato, sliced

1 gherkin/pickle, chopped

½ red onion, sliced

a handful of fresh
coriander/cilantro

1–2 tablespoons freshly
squeezed lime juice

*a baking sheet lined with
baking parchment*

makes 5 burgers

*This is my go-to veggie burger! Quinoa is moist and mixes with
sweet potato and black beans to give a meaty consistency. This
vegetarian burger will satisfy the carnivore in all of us.*

Preheat the oven to 180ºC (350ºF) Gas 4.

Heat 1 tablespoon of the olive oil in a saucepan or pot over medium heat.
Fry the onions for about 3 minutes, until softened. Add the garlic and
cook for another minute. Then add the beans, stir and cook for a few
minutes longer. Remove from the heat and transfer the mixture to a large
mixing bowl.

Lightly mash the beans with a fork until they're semi-crushed. Add the
rest of the ingredients (except the mushrooms and remaining olive oil) to
the bowl and mix well. If the mixture is too moist, add extra breadcrumbs.
If too dry, add some more smashed beans.

Form patties with your hands and place on the prepared baking sheet.
Bake in the preheated oven for 20–25 minutes, checking after about 15
minutes and turning once to insure even browning. Once cooked remove
from the main oven and keep warm in a cool oven or hot plate.

Increase the temperature of the oven to 200ºC (400ºF) Gas 6.

For the mushroom base, clean the mushrooms with a damp cloth.
Remove the stems and drizzle with the remaining 2 tablespoons olive oil.
Season with salt and pepper and roast for 20 minutes.

When ready to serve, place each burger on top of a roasted mushroom
and garnish with your choice of traditional burger toppings.

*Note: To prepare a basic cooked quinoa, put 210 g/1 cup quinoa in a frying
pan/skillet with 240 ml/1 cup stock and 200 ml/1 cup water. Bring to the
boil then reduce the temperature. Cover and simmer for 20 minutes.
Uncover, fluff with a fork and set aside for 5 minutes before using.*

herb & seed crusted tilapia with bulgur & green pea purée

140 g/1 cup bulgur
480 ml/2 cups vegetable
  stock
2 tilapia fillets
2 tablespoons olive oil

herb crust
1 teaspoon hulled hemp
  seeds
15 g/¼ cup panko crumbs
  (or gluten-free
  breadcrumbs)
¼ teaspoon salt
1 short sprig of rosemary,
  leaves stripped
1 teaspoon chopped fresh
  chives

pea purée
120 g/1 cup fresh peas,
  shelled
50 g/2 large handfuls baby
  spinach
120 ml/½ cup water
a small handful of freshly
  chopped mint
¼ teaspoon salt

*a baking sheet lined with
  baking parchment*

serves 2

A bright green purée can make any dish stand out. Bulgur is an ancient grain that has more fibre than rice. It's made from cracked wheat and is a quick-cooking grain which is great for those who are just starting to incorporate more wholegrains into their diet. If you are following a gluten-free diet, warm quinoa (see page 91) is the perfect substitute for the bulgur here.

Preheat the oven to 180°C (350°F) Gas 4.

Put the bulgur and vegetable stock in a saucepan or pot over a medium–high heat. Bring to the boil, then reduce the heat, cover, and simmer for 20 minutes. Uncover, fluff with a fork, return the lid and set aside.

Rinse and pat the tilapia filets dry with paper towels or a clean, dry cloth, then place them on the prepared baking sheet.

For the herb crust, mix the hemp seeds, panko crumbs, salt and herbs on a large plate. Sprinkle the crust on top of the fillets, so the fillets are covered. Drizzle with olive oil and bake in the preheated oven for 15 minutes.

While the fish is cooking make the pea purée. Fill a second saucepan or pot with water and bring to the boil over a high heat. Add the peas and cook for around 3 minutes, until they are tender. Transfer the peas to a food processor using a slotted spoon. Blanch the spinach in the same boiling water for about a minute, then add the spinach to the peas. Purée the spinach and peas with the water, mint and salt. Set aside.

To serve, spoon the purée onto a plate, next to the bulgur and set the fish on top. Serve immediately.

poppy seed-crusted salmon with a tropical ratatouille

2 tablespoons poppy seeds

3 tablespoons panko crumbs (or gluten-free breadcrumbs)

1 teaspoon paprika

1 tablespoon olive oil

1 garlic clove, crushed

2 salmon fillets

sea salt and freshly ground black pepper

a handful of chopped flat-leaf parsley, to garnish

tropical ratatouille

2 tablespoons olive oil

1 teaspoon salt, plus extra to taste

1 red onion, diced

2 garlic cloves, crushed

2 teaspoons deseeded and chopped green jalapeño chillies

½ yellow pepper, chopped

1 teaspoon chilli powder

1 teaspoon paprika

130 g/1 cup diced swede

1 courgette/zucchini, sliced

1 yellow summer squash, sliced

4 tomatoes, chopped

1 mango, peeled, stoned and chopped

a baking sheet lined with baking parchment

Roasted salmon was a staple in my diet growing up. My mom called it 'brain food' long before the benefits of fish oils were written about in popular magazines. Poppy seeds are a healthy addition and look great as well. Ratatouille is a classic French dish, but instead of traditional French herbs, I like to put in a kick with some jalapeño and temper it with mango to give a brighter taste.

Preheat the oven to 180°C (350°F) Gas 4.

To make the ratatouille, set a large frying pan/skillet over medium heat, add 1 tablespoon of the olive oil, the salt and red onion and fry for about 3 minutes or until the onion is translucent. Add the garlic, jalapeño chilli, paprika, yellow pepper, chilli powder and paprika, and cook for a further minute. Then add the swede and remaining olive oil. Cook for 10 minutes, stirring occasionally. Next, add the courgette/zucchini with the summer squash and mango and cook for a further 5 minutes. Add the chopped tomatoes and continue to cook, stirring occasionally, for a further 8 minutes. Season with more salt, if required.

Meanwhile, in a small bowl, mix together the poppy seeds, panko crumbs, paprika, olive oil, and garlic to form a crust.

Rinse and pat the salmon fillets dry with paper towels or a clean, dry cloth, then place them on the prepared baking sheet. Season with salt and black pepper and spoon the poppy seed crust evenly onto each salmon fillet. Bake in the preheated oven for 15 minutes (or slightly longer if the fillets are very thick).

Serve the salmon with a generous spoonful of the ratatouille and garnish with flat-leaf parsley.

sea bass with red quinoa & fennel courgette salad

190 g/1 cup red quinoa

460 ml/scant 2 cups water

¼ teaspoon salt

1 teaspoon butter

2 tablespoons olive oil

1 large fennel bulb, chopped, with fronds reserved to garnish

2 courgettes/zucchini, peeled in strips and chopped

leaves from 2 sprigs of fresh oregano

2 garlic cloves

2 x 140-g/5-oz skinless sea bass fillets

2 tablespoons vegetable stock

serves 2

Red quinoa is better at holding its shape and has a slightly chrunchier texture than white, which pairs nicely with light white fish like sea bass.

Put the red quinoa and water in a medium saucepan or pot and bring to the boil over a high heat. Reduce the heat, cover, and simmer for 20 minutes. Remove from the heat, uncover, fluff with a fork, then stir in the salt and butter, and set aside.

While the quinoa is cooking, heat the olive oil in a large frying pan/skillet over a medium heat. Add the fennel and courgette/zucchini and fry for 5 minutes. Turn the heat down to medium, then add the oregano, garlic and salt, and cook for a further 5 minutes. Nestle the sea bass fillets in the pan, add the vegetable stock. Reduce the heat, cover and poach for 5 minutes. Then turn off the heat and set aside for another 3 minutes to ensure the sea bass is fully cooked.

To serve, spoon a mound of quinoa on a plate. Plate the cooked sea bass with the fennel, courgettes/zucchini and juice from the pan on top. Garnish with fennel fronds and enjoy immediately.

quinoa spaghetti with chilli crab

125 g/5 oz dry quinoa
spaghetti
2 garlic cloves, crushed
2 tablespoons olive oil
400 g/1⅓ cups chopped
tomatoes
a pinch of dried chilli/hot
red pepper flakes
80 g/½ cup fresh white
crab meat
Himalayan salt and freshly
ground black pepper,
to taste
a handful of fresh flat-leaf
parsley, to garnish

serves 2

This recipe is one of my husband's favourites. I always forget how easy it is to make. In London, portion sizes are small, so it was easy to get a small pot of fresh white crab meat that was perfect for cooking for two.

Bring a large saucepan or pot of water to the boil over a high heat. Add the quinoa spaghetti and cook according to the packet instructions.

While the spaghetti is cooking, fry the garlic in the olive oil in a medium–large frying pan/skillet over a medium heat until the garlic just begins to turn brown. Then add the chopped tomatoes and dried chilli/hot red pepper flakes and cook for another few minutes. Reduce the heat and add the crab meat just to warm through.

Drain the spaghetti and put it in the same pan as the sauce. Gently mix the crab and tomato sauce with the spaghetti.

Serve the spaghetti on plates or in large pasta bowls, adding salt and pepper to taste, and garnish with chopped flat-leaf parsley.

sesame seared tuna with asian slaw

40 g/⅓ cup mixed black
and white sesame seeds
2 x 170-g/6-oz sushi grade
tuna pieces
2 tablespoons grapeseed oil
sea salt and freshly ground
black pepper

for the asian slaw
250 g/1 cup jícama, sliced
in long strips
½ mango, sliced in long
strips
100 g/2 packed cups thinly
sliced red cabbage

tamari sauce
1 tablespoon soy sauce
(check for gluten-free)
2 teaspoons sesame oil
¼ teaspoon finely sliced
ginger
2 teaspoons flaxseed oil
2 teaspoons clear honey
1 tablespoon freshly
squeezed lemon juice
1 tablespoon white sesame
seeds
a handful of fresh
coriander/cilantro,
to garnish

serves 4

When my son was a toddler, I gave him a piece of jícama. I described it as a 'white watermelon' and he devoured it. Sometimes you have to stretch the truth a bit to introduce new foods but jícama is a great vegetable on its own and, as here, in coleslaw. Walk into your local sushi chain and it's easy to see that sesame seeds are often used for presentation. But they actually give a nutritional punch of calcium and magnesium as well!

Spread the black and white sesame seeds evenly on a plate. Season each side of tuna with salt and pepper. Then coat each side of the tuna with the seed mixture – don't forget the sides as well. In a grill pan, heat the grapeseed oil over medium–high heat. Once the oil is hot, sear the tuna for 30 seconds on all 4 sides. Remove from the pan and set aside.

For the asian slaw, cut the jícama, mango and cabbage into long strips.

Whisk all the ingredients for the tamari sauce together in a bowl. Add the slaw and mix it all together.

To serve, thinly slice the tuna steak. Spoon a generous amount of slaw on each plate and place the sliced tuna on top. Garnish with fresh coriander/cilantro.

seared scallops with red rice & ginger almond sauce

12 scallops
3 tablespoons olive oil
freshly squeezed juice
    of ½ of a lemon
sea salt and freshly ground
    black pepper, to taste
the green of 1 spring
    onion/scallion,
    to garnish

bhutanese red rice
360 ml/1½ cups water
190 g/1 cup Bhutanese
    red rice
1 tablespoon butter
a pinch of sea salt

sauce
½ onion, chopped
2 tablespoons grapeseed oil
1 tablespoon grated ginger
2 garlic cloves, crushed
30 g/¼ cup flaked/slivered
    almonds
2 tablespoons almond milk
1½ teaspoons soy sauce
2 teaspoons clear honey

serves 2

There are many different kinds of red rice. Each one has a different cooking time, so it is important to check the instructions on the packet. Bhutanese red rice is a good option here because it still has some of the bran layer in tact and cooks quickly. The ginger almond sauce is a great Asian accompaniment to any fish.

First, cook the rice. Bring the water to the boil in a large saucepan or pot over a high heat. Add the rice and reduce the heat. Cover and simmer for 20 minutes. Then add the butter and salt, and stir until melted.

Rinse and pat the scallops dry with paper towels or a clean, dry cloth. Season each side with salt and pepper. Add the olive oil to a large pan set over a high heat. Place the scallops in the pan being careful not to overcrowd them. Cook for 3–5 minutes, until golden brown then turn them over and cook for a further 2 minutes.

For the sauce, fry the onion in 1 tablespoon of grapeseed oil in a non-stick pan for 10 minutes over high heat. Reduce the heat, add the ginger, garlic and almonds, and fry for a further 5 minutes. Transfer to a food processor, add the almond milk, soy sauce, honey and the second tablespoon of grapeseed oil, and blend.

To serve, spoon the rice and ginger almond sauce onto a plate. Place 6 scallops on each plate and drizzle with lemon juice. Garnish with chopped spring onion/scallion.

saffron shrimp with barley pilaf

1 onion, chopped
2 tablespoons plus
   1 teaspoon vegetable oil
1 garlic clove, crushed
200 g/1 cup hull-less
   barley
240 ml/1 cup water
480 ml/2 cups vegetable
   stock
1 bay leaf
12 medium uncooked
   prawns/shrimp, peeled
   and deveined
1 teaspoon paprika
1 teaspoon turmeric
1 teaspoon ground
   cinnamon
1 teaspoon ground
   cardamom
a pinch of saffron threads
a handful of fresh flat-leaf
   parsley, to garnish

serves 2

Like rice, there are many forms of barley. Hull-less barley has most of its outer layer in tact so it is considered a wholegrain. Pearl barley has had its outer layer completely removed so it does not earn its place as a coveted super grain and does not have the same health benefits. The bran layer contains the fibre, vitamins and protein. Barley is chewy and mild tasting so it is very versatile. It's great in soups, salads and pilafs. However, it is not gluten-free so I recommend substituting brown basmati rice for this dish.

In a medium saucepan or pot, fry the onion in 2 tablespoons of vegetable oil for 4–5 minutes over high heat. Reduce the heat, then add the garlic and barley, toasting for 3 minutes. Then add the water, stock and bay leaf. Bring to the boil, then cover and simmer for about 50 minutes. The grains will be softened and chewy when fully cooked.

In a separate medium non-stick frying pan/skillet, heat 1 teaspoon of vegetable oil over a medium heat and add the paprika, turmeric, cinnamon, cardamom and saffron. Add the prawns/shrimp and fry for 3 minutes on each side, or until they are completely opaque.

Remove the bay leaf from the barley and scoop a generous amount and 6 prawns/shrimp on each plate. Garnish with fresh flat-leaf parsley.

cold poached salmon with cucumber quinoa salad

1 unwaxed lemon, sliced
120 ml/½ cup water
120 ml/½ cup white wine
500 g/2 salmon fillets
1 tablespoon capers
3 small cucumbers, diced
2 tablespoons finely sliced
   red onion, soaked in
   water for 10 minutes
½ yellow bell pepper,
   chopped
15 g/8 tablespoons
   chopped dill
2 tablespoons chopped
   chives
280 g/2 cups cooked
   quinoa (see page 91)
Himalayan salt and freshly
   ground black pepper,
   to taste

dressing
4 tablespoons extra virgin
   olive oil
2 tablespoons champagne
   vinegar
freshly squeezed juice
   of 1 clementine

serves 2

This dish makes me think of a summer garden party. It's colourful, healthy, and so easy to entertain with. Prepare everything the day before and set it out before your guests arrive.

Put 4 slices of lemon, water and white wine in a large frying pan/skillet. Place the salmon fillets on top of the lemon slices, skin side down. Bring the liquid to a simmer over a medium–high heat. Turn the heat to low, cover and cook for 5 minutes. Then turn off the heat, and let the fish continue to sit on the stove for a further 5 minutes while it continues to cook. This is a good way to prevent it from overcooking.

Transfer the salmon fillets to a plate, reserving the poaching liquid.

Add the capers, salt and pepper to the poaching liquid and reduce by half over a medium heat to make a sauce. Drizzle the sauce over the salmon, cover and chill in the refrigerator.

In a large mixing bowl, mix together the cucumber, red onion, yellow pepper, 1 tablespoon each of the dill and chives, and the cooked quinoa. Make the dressing by whisking all of the ingredients together. Then drizzle over the quinoa salad and store in the refrigerator.

When you are ready to serve, plate the salmon with the quinoa salad and garnish with the reserved dill and chives.

moroccan chicken tagine with brown lentils

2 teaspoons olive oil

1 teaspoon cumin

1 teaspoon ground coriander

a pinch of sea salt

a pinch of freshly ground black pepper

a drizzle of vegetable oil

2 chicken breasts, bone and skin kept on

1 onion, chopped

250 ml/1 cup chicken stock

6–8 dried whole Turkish apricots, soaked in water for 10 minutes

1 orange, peeled and cut in wedges

8 pitted green olives

2 garlic cloves, crushed

1 teaspoon cinnamon

190 g/1 cup dried green or brown lentils

480 ml/2 cups water

a handful of fresh flat-leaf parsley, to garnish

serves 2

My trip to Marrakesh was a spice adventure. The maze of spice shops in the souks was exhilarating. I like to cook the lentils separately or use store-bought, pre-cooked lentils, which make this dish easier to do on a weeknight. If you don't have a tagine, a cast iron pot or Dutch oven work well too! But the presentation of a tagine gives a dramatic touch when entertaining!

First, mix the olive oil, cumin, coriander, cardamom, salt and pepper in a bowl. Then scoop the spice mixture under the chicken skin breast, as evenly as possible, coating the two breasts. Reserve any excess mixture.

In a large stove-top tagine, heat the vegetable oil on medium–high heat. Then add chicken, skin side down to brown the skin, and cook for 5 minutes. Remove the chicken and set aside. Remove any excess chicken fat but leave a little to coat the base of the tagine.

In the same tagine, add the onion with half of the chicken stock and fry for 8 minutes, or until the onion is translucent. Add the chicken, skin side up, the soaked apricots, orange wedges and olives, and the rest of the spice mixture. Turn the heat to low and cook for 40 minutes.

Rinse the dried lentils. Then put them in a separate medium saucepan or pot over a high heat with the water. Bring to the boil, then reduce the heat and simmer, uncovered for 30–40 minutes, adding water if required so the lentils are always just covered.

Remove the chicken from the tagine and cover in foil to keep warm. Then add the cooked lentils, the remaining 60 ml/¼ cup of chicken stock and mix together with the apricots, orange wedges and olives, making sure everything is mixed together and hot.

Using a slotted spoon, plate a generous scoop of the lentil mixture and put the chicken on top. Drizzle with a little extra sauce from the pan and garnish with fresh flat-leaf parsley.

roast chicken with chia chimichuri

2 chicken breasts, bone
  and skin kept on
1 unwaxed lemon, sliced
4 garlic cloves, 1 crushed
  and 3 whole
a handful of fresh flat-leaf
  parsley
a drizzle of olive oil
sea salt and freshly ground
  black pepper, to taste

chimichuri sauce
2 tablespoons red wine
  vinegar
2 handfuls fresh parsley
2 handfuls fresh
  coriander/cilantro
1 garlic clove, crushed
1 shallot
½ cup olive oil
freshly squeezed juice
  of ½ a lemon
a pinch of dried chilli/hot
  red pepper flakes
50 g/½ cup spinach
2 tablespoons milled chia
  seeds
sea salt and freshly ground
  black pepper, to taste

serves 2

My sister in law makes a delicious chimichuri sauce and I've now come to expect her special spicy concoction for our Californian family dinners. You can't even tell that chia seeds are blended in this sauce. Since its green, you can really be creative with throwing in various super greens too!

Preheat the oven to 180ºC (350ºF) Gas 4.

Prepare the chicken breasts on a plate. Pull away the skin so you can make a little pocket for the seasonings. In each pocket, put in one or two slices of lemon, the crushed garlic, salt, pepper and fresh parsley. Lay the remaining lemon slices in a non-stick roasting pan with the whole garlic cloves. Put the chicken breasts on top, drizzle with olive oil and roast the chicken in the preheated oven for 40 minutes.

For the chimichuri sauce, blend all of the ingredients in a food processor and adjust the seasoning with salt and pepper to taste.

Serve with your favourite wholegrain or salad.

thai chicken & fruit curry with brown rice

190 g/1 cup short grain
  brown rice
480 ml/2 cups water
1 onion, finely chopped
2 tablespoons vegetable
  oil
2 teaspoons finely chopped
  fresh ginger
2 lemongrass stalks,
  chopped (bottom white
  part only)
2 garlic cloves, crushed
2 tablespoons Thai red
  curry paste
2 skinless and boneless
  chicken breasts, diced
60 g/½ cup pineapple
  chunks
60 g/½ cup mango, diced
400 ml/1¾ cups low-fat
  coconut milk
120 ml/½ cup water
freshly squeezed juice
  of 1 lime
sea salt and freshly ground
  black pepper, to taste

serves 2

The flavour combination of fruit, spice and coconut is a favourite of mine. If you can't get hold of lemongrass, this will still be delicious as store-bought curry paste is loaded with flavour.

Cook the rice in the water in a saucepan or pot over a medium–high heat. Bring the water to the boil then reduce the temperature. Cover and simmer on a low heat for 30 minutes.

In a large non-stick pan, stir fry the onion, ginger and lemongrass in the vegetable oil for 5 minutes on a medium–high heat. Then add the garlic and curry paste, stirring continuously for 1 minute. Add the chicken to the pan and brown on all sides. Then add the pineapple and mango and cook for 5 minutes. Finally, add the coconut milk and water. Reduce the temperature and cook uncovered for 15 minutes.

At the end, season with salt, pepper and lime juice, to taste, and serve with the cooked brown rice.

1 onion, finely chopped
2 garlic cloves, crushed
1 tablespoon olive oil
900 g/2 lbs ground turkey
1 large carrot, finely grated
60 ml/½ cup gluten-free
    barbecue sauce
30 ml/¼ cup ketchup
2 eggs
60 g/½ cup millet flour
the leaves from 2 sprigs
    of fresh thyme
2 sage leaves, chopped
1 teaspoon Himalayan salt
1 teaspoon ground white
    pepper
2 tablespoons balsamic
    vinegar

broccolini
400 g/14 oz broccolini
2 garlic cloves, crushed
1½ tablespoons olive oil
½ teaspoon sea salt
¼ teaspoon freshly ground
    black pepper

millet mash
1 small onion
1 tablespoon olive oil
2 garlic cloves, crushed
1 parsnip, peeled and
    chopped
190 g/1 cup millet grain
600 ml/2½ cups vegetable
    stock
120 ml/½ cup water

*a loaf pan lined with
    baking parchment*

serves 4-6

turkey meatloaf with millet mash & broccolini

This is a creative way to use millet in two different forms with two very different outcomes. I use millet flour as the binding agent in the meatloaf and then as an alternative to mashed potatoes, I cook millet and puree it with a parsnip to form a mash.

Preheat the oven to 180ºC (350ºF) Gas 4.

In a medium frying pan/skillet, fry the onion and garlic in olive oil for a few minutes, until the onion is translucent. Set aside in a bowl to cool.

In a large mixing bowl, mix the ground turkey, carrot, barbecue sauce, ketchup, millet flour, eggs, herbs, salt and pepper. Mix together with the cooled onion and garlic. Then spoon the mixture into the prepared loaf pan. Bake in the preheated oven for 50 minutes. During the last 20 minutes of cooking, brush the top with balsamic vinegar twice.

Lay the broccolini on a baking sheet. Sprinkle over the garlic, drizzle with olive oil and season with salt and pepper. Roast in the oven with the meatloaf for the last 30 minutes of cooking time, turning once.

For the millet mash, fry the onion in olive oil in a saucepan or pot over a medium–high heat for 5–8 minutes or until translucent. Add the garlic and chopped parsnip, and fry for a further 2 minutes. Then add the millet, vegetable stock and water and bring to the boil. Reduce the temperature, cover and simmer for 20 minutes. Purée the millet mash in a food processor.

To serve, scoop out a generous helping of mash, then place slices of the meatloaf on top with the broccolini to the side.

lamb kebab with buckwheat tabouli

2 tablespoons olive oil

1 teaspoon ground cumin

½ teaspoon salt

1 teaspoon paprika

1 teaspoon ground coriander

550 g/1½ lbs lamb shoulder or leg, cut into cubes

8 cherry tomatoes

8 button mushrooms

buckwheat tabouli

185 g/1 cup dry buckwheat

240 ml/1 cup vegetable stock

240 ml/1 cup water

1 medium tomato, chopped

1 small cucumber, chopped

1 spring onion/scallion, finely chopped

20 g/⅛ cup finely chopped fresh mint

45 g/½ cup chopped flat-leaf parsley

3 tablespoons freshly squeezed lemon juice

2 tablespoons olive oil

1 teaspoon Himalayan salt

4 metal skewers

serves 2

I recommend befriending your local butcher. That way when it comes down to a specific cut of meat and size, it's easy to have it done for you and you know exactly where your meat is coming from! Tabouli is traditionally made with bulgur, but if you're following a gluten-free diet, buckwheat is a great alternative grain that would be delicious here.

First prepare a marinade for the lamb. Whisk the olive oil, cumin, salt, paprika and ground coriander together in a bowl. Add the lamb pieces and stir well to coat the meat. Transfer the coated lamb to a food bag and leave to marinate for 30 minute.

For the buckwheat tabouli, put the vegetable stock, water, and buckwheat in a large saucepan or pot. Set over a high heat and bring to a boil. Reduce the temperature and simmer for 15 minutes with the lid half on, stirring once in between. Be careful not to overcook the grains. Transfer to a sieve/strainer and rinse with cold water then set aside in a bowl to cool.

Once cooled, stir through the tomato, cucumber, spring onions/scallion, mint, parsley, lemon juice and olive oil. Season with salt and set in the refrigerator until you are ready to serve.

Build the kebabs by threading a piece of lamb, a cherry tomato, and button mushroom, alternating in this pattern, so each skewer has 4 pieces of lamb.

Put the skewers on a grill pan over a medium–high heat and grill for approximately 4 minutes on each side.

Serve 2 lamb skewers per portion with a generous amount of tabouli.

lamb chops with warm apricot quinoa

Warm white quinoa is my comfort food. I always love how Moroccan food mixes fruit into meat dishes. Here, I've mixed the quinoa with fresh apricots, which are delicious with lamb. Turkish dried apricots soaked in water for 10 minutes will work just as well if fresh apricots aren't in season.

6 lamb chops (¾-in thick)
185 g/1 cup dry quinoa
240 ml/1 cup water
210 ml/1 scant cup
    vegetable stock
2 tablespoons plus
    1 teaspoon olive oil
1 small onion, chopped
1 garlic clove, crushed
2 teaspoons jalapeño,
    chopped and deseeded
20 g/⅛ cup currants
60 g/½ cup apricots,
    chopped (if using dried,
    soak 50 g/⅓ cup in water
    for 10 minutes, then
    chop)
a handful of freshly
    chopped coriander/
    cilantro
freshly squeezed juice
    of 1 lime
1 teaspoon dried cumin
2 teaspoons paprika
½ teaspoon chilli powder
1 tablespoon ground
    coriander
sea salt and freshly ground
    black pepper

serves 4–6

Before you start, take the lamb chops out of the refrigerator to bring them to room temperature.

Put the quinoa and water in a medium saucepan or pot and bring to the boil over a high heat. Reduce the heat, cover, and simmer for 20 minutes. Remove from the heat, uncover, fluff with a fork and set aside.

Once the quinoa is cooked, heat 1 tablespoon of olive oil in a large frying pan/skillet over medium–high heat and fry the onion for 5–8 minutes until translucent. Reduce the heat slightly, then add the garlic and jalapeño and cook for 2 minutes. Add 1 teaspoon of olive oil, the cooked quinoa, currants and apricots, and toss to combine. Transfer the mixture to a serving dish. Season with salt and pepper, scatter coriander/cilantro across the dish and drizzle with lime juice.

Prepare a coating for the lamb. Mix all of the spices in a bowl. Then rub the lamb chops with the mixture, coating each side. Heat 1 tablespoon of olive oil in a grill pan. Add the lamb chops and grill for 3 minutes on each side to cook medium-rare and slightly longer for well done. Remove from the heat and leave to rest for 5 minutes. Serve with the warm quinoa.

seared steak with amaranth asparagus risotto

2 x 450 g/8-oz sirloin
  steaks
¼ teaspoon onion powder
  or ¼ small onion, finely
  chopped
1 teaspoon paprika
½ teaspoon chipotle
  powder
1 tablespoon olive oil
80 ml/⅓ cup dry red wine
1 shallot, chopped
60 ml/¼ cup chicken stock

risotto
1 tablespoon olive oil
1 large onion, chopped
2 garlic cloves, chopped
170 g/1 cup amaranth
240 ml/1 cup water
240 ml/1 cup vegetable
  stock
sea salt and freshly ground
  black pepper

serves 2

Amaranth, one of our prized ancient grains, can be made into a hearty warm side dish. I call it a 'risotto' because of its smooth and creamy consistency. For a vegetarian option you could serve the risotto with chunks of seasoned tofu.

Before you start, take the steaks out of the refrigerator to bring them to room temperature.

Heat the olive oil in a large frying pan/skillet over medium–high heat and fry the onion for 5–8 minutes until translucent. Reduce the heat slightly, then add the garlic and cook for a further 2 minutes. Then add the amaranth, with the water and vegetable stock. Bring to the boil then reduce the heat. Cover and simmer for 15 minutes. Then add the asparagus tips and cook uncovered for another 10 minutes, stirring occasionally, until you have a thick and creamy consistency. Season with salt and pepper to taste.

While the risotto is cooking, prepare the steak. Mix together the onion powder, paprika and chipotle powder on a plate. Generously season the steaks with salt and pepper on both sides. Then rub the spice mixture into the steaks, covering all sides.

Heat the olive oil in a large saucepan or pot over medium–high heat. Add the steak and sear for 4–5 minutes on each side. Transfer the steak to a warmed plate and cover with foil to keep warm.

To make a serving sauce, add the wine, the shallot and the stock to the pan used to cook the steak and bring to the boil. Cook for 4 minutes to reduce the liquid by half. Season the sauce with salt and pepper and transfer to a jug.

Slice the steak and serve with the risotto and red wine sauce.

desserts & sweet treats

You can have your cake and eat it too
with these healthy and delicious recipes
to end the perfect meal.

2 eggs (see Note)

200 ml/1 cup coconut milk

70 g/½ cup vegetable oil

300 g/2 cups melted dark
  semisweet chocolate

1 teaspoon vanilla extract

40 g/⅓ cup brown rice
  flour

40 g/⅓ cup teff flour

45 g/⅓ cup potato starch

2 tablespoons flaxseeds

1 teaspoon xanthan gum

¾ teaspoon baking powder

¾ teaspoon bicarbonate of
  soda/baking soda

50 g/½ cup cocoa powder

1 teaspoon espresso
  powder

100 g/½ cup coconut sugar

almond butter icing

80 ml/⅓ cup coconut oil

60 ml/¼ cup smooth
  unsalted almond butter

375 g/3 cups icing/
  confectioners' sugar

3–6 teaspoons almond
  milk

1 teaspoon vanilla extract

*a muffin pan lined with
  paper cases*

makes 9 cupcakes

chocolate cupcakes with almond butter icing

Ah, you can have your cake and eat it too! Here is a rich chocolate cupcake using a high percentage of wholegrain flour as its base.

Preheat the oven to 180°C (350°F) Gas 4.

Put all of the wet ingredients into a mixing bowl and whisk until smooth. Sift the dry ingredients into a separate mixing bowl then add the wet to the dry mixture a little at a time. Whisk until completely smooth and mixed together. Spoon the mix into the prepared muffin pan. Bake for 20 minutes until a toothpick comes out clean. Leave to cool on a wire rack.

For the icing, beat the coconut oil and almond butter together very quickly until well combined. Add 125 g/1 cup of the icing/confectioners' sugar with a teaspoon of almond milk and stir in slowly. Add the vanilla extract and continue to add a little of the sugar and a teaspoon of milk to the mixture at a time, keeping the consistency thick and fluffy.

Note: If you prefer not to use eggs you could use egg replacer or make a flax-egg mix by combining 2 tablespoons of ground flaxseed with 6 tablespoons of water.

puffed seeded bark

30 g/¼ cup pumpkin seeds

30 g/¼ cup toasted sesame
seeds

38 g/1½ cup puffed
amaranth or puffed
millet

450 g/1¾ cups (70 %) dark
chocolate broken into
rough pieces

75 g/½ cup dried cherries
or cranberries

*a baking sheet lined with
parchment paper*

serves 6

*Chocolate bark is a fun dessert. It also makes a great gift when
wrapped in little transparent bags. The messy part of me likes that
it looks perfect broken up into any size pieces and it's great to make
with kids! In the UK, puffed amaranth is readily available whereas
in the States, puffed millet is a much easier find. Either works!*

Preheat the oven to 180ºC (350ºF) Gas 4.

Scatter the pumpkin seeds across a baking sheet and toast for about 10
minutes, until fragrant. Remove from the oven and set aside to cool.

Melt the dark chocolate in a bowl set over a pan of boiling water. Stir
until smooth. Remove the bowl from the pan, add the vanilla extract and
fold in the puffed amaranth. Spread the mixture onto the prepared
baking sheet as evenly as possible. Top the melted chocolate rectangle
with the toasted pumpkin seeds, sunflower seeds, and dried cherries. Put
in the refrigerator for 40 minutes to set, until the chocolate is firm.

Break into pieces and enjoy!

coconut chia pudding

40 g/¼ cup chia seeds
1 teaspoon vanilla extract
¼ teaspoon coconut
   extract (available online)
1 tablespoon cashew butter
300 ml/1¼ cup coconut
   milk
1 teaspoon cinnamon
2 tablespoons shredded
   coconut, plus 1
   tablespoon, to garnish
2 tablespoons jam, to serve
   (optional)

serves 2

My idea of fun is taking a superfood and making dessert from it so that my family can have treats that I feel good about. This was the reason why I first developed my baking mixes and the reason why I always have guilt-free desserts in my kitchen. My husband had a white rice pudding phase and I had to figure out a way to satisfy this craving, so I swapped out the white rice for chia seeds, and he hasn't asked for rice pudding since! Cashew butter gives this dessert a subtle warmth, but I've done this with peanut butter and it's just as delicious!

Put the chia seeds aside in a large mixing bowl. Mix the rest of the ingredients together in a food processor. Then pour the mixture into the mixing bowl with the chia seeds and stir with a fork. Set aside and then stir again after 10 minutes.

Put in the refrigerator to set. The pudding will be firm after an hour but can be left to set overnight.

When ready to serve, sprinkle shredded coconut over each pudding and add a dollop of your favourite fruit jam.

spice cake with mesquite flour

Mesquite flour is made from grinding mesquite pods. It has a smoky, nutty and sweet flavour that pairs perfectly with cinnamon. I fell in love with its unique aroma immediately and it's now readily available in health food stores as a gluten-free alternative to wheat flour. It's best mixed with other flours because it has such a dominant flavour. You can add a scoop of this flour to your pancake batter too!

3 egg whites and 2 egg yolks
140 g/1 cup potato starch
50 g/½ cup quinoa flour
65 g/½ cup teff flour
75 g/¾ cup mesquite flour
2 teaspoons xanthan gum
1 teaspoon bicarbonate of soda/
   baking soda
1½ teaspoons baking powder
½ teaspoon sea salt

3 teaspoons cinnamon
1 teaspoon nutmeg
¼ teaspoon ground cloves
150 ml/¾ cup vegetable oil
140 g/1 cup sugar, xylitol or other sugar
   substitute
300 g/1¼ cups apple purée/sauce

a 23-cm/9-in cake pan lined with baking
   parchment

makes 16

Preheat the oven to 180ºC (350ºF) Gas 4.

Beat the egg whites to soft peaks and set aside. Whisk all of the dry ingredients together. Then in a separate bowl, beat the vegetable oil, sugar, apple purée/sauce and egg yolks together. Beat the wet and dry ingredients together to form a smooth batter. Then gently fold in the egg whites and softly whisk the mixture until completely mixed.

Pour the batter into the prepared cake pan. Bake in the preheated oven for 35 minutes or until a metal skewer comes out clean from the centre. Leave to cool in the pan before turning out.

yogurt panna cotta with an oat crumble

Panna Cotta is my favourite Italian dessert. I love its thick, cool consistency. I use wholegrains for the crumble topping here and the coconut sugar gives the panna cotta a tan hue and a deep caramel flavour.

120 ml/½ cup light
   coconut milk
65g/½ cup coconut sugar,
   sugar, xylitol or other
   sugar substitute
1 teaspoon vanilla extract
3 teaspoons gelatin powder
6 tablespoons water
120 ml/½ cup plain full-fat
   yogurt
60 ml/¼ cup full-fat
   coconut milk
a handful of raspberries

crumble topping:
30g/¼ cup quinoa flour
1 tablespoon milled
   flaxseeds
3 tablespoons coconut sugar
90g/¾ cup rolled oats
a pinch of salt
60 ml/¼ cup coconut oil,
   melted

4 ramekins

serves 4

In a saucepan, gently heat the light coconut milk, coconut sugar and vanilla extract until the sugar dissolves.

While the milk is heating, put the gelatin in the water. Set aside for 5 minutes to thicken. Add the gelatin to the hot milk liquid and stir until it dissolves. Leave to cool.

Once cool, stir the yogurt into the mixture and whisk in the full-fat coconut milk. Pour into individual ramekins and chill in the refrigerator for 2 hours.

For the crumble topping, preheat the oven to 180ºC (350ºF) Gas 4.

Combine the quinoa flour, flaxseeds, coconut sugar and oats with a pinch of salt in a mixing bowl. Then, using your fingers, work in the melted coconut oil. Spread onto a baking sheet and bake in the preheated oven for 20 minutes.

Serve the panna cotta with a sprinkling of topping and a few fresh raspberries, or, if you prefer, you could turn the panna cotta out onto a dessert plate. The easiest way to do this is to dip the bottom of the ramekin in hot water for 5–10 seconds, place a plate on top of the dessert and turn over to remove the ramekin upside down.

vegan chocolate fudge cake

30 g/¼ cup sorghum flour

30 g/¼ cup teff flour

35 g/¼ cup potato starch

1½ teaspoons baking powder

½ teaspoon bicarbonate of soda/baking soda

½ teaspoon salt

3 tablespoons milled flaxseeds

230 ml/1 cup coffee

95 ml/½ cup agave plus 95 ml/¼ cup xylitol or other sugar substitute

2 teaspoons lemon juice

60 g/⅔ cup cocoa powder

95 ml/½ cup vegetable oil

1 tablespoon vanilla extract

1 teaspoon xanthan gum

an 23-cm/9-in cake pan, greased and dusted with almond flour

serves 8

It's always nice to have a vegan dessert recipe on hand. Sorghum is another ancient grain from the grass species that is commonly used as a gluten-free flour. It is a good base flour, since it pairs well with other flours and has little flavour. Freekeh flour is another ancient grain, now more prevalently used as flour, that could be used here.

Preheat the oven to 180ºC (350ºF) Gas 4.

Sift the sorghum flour, teff flour and potato starch together in a large mixing bowl. Add the baking powder, bicarbonate of soda/baking soda and salt to the sifted flours and mix.

In a separate bowl, whisk the flaxseeds together with the coffee. Add the remaining wet ingredients to the flax–coffee mix and stir together.

Add the dry mixture to the wet and whisk until fully combined. Pour into the prepared cake pan and bake in the preheated oven for 25 minutes until a knife comes out clean from the centre.

Serve immediately and enjoy.

peach pie with sunflower crust

145 g/1 cup sunflower
    seeds
60 g/½ cup quinoa flour
40 g/⅓ cup potato starch
60 g/⅓ cup sugar
¼ teaspoon sea salt
7 tablespoons melted
    coconut oil

filling
8 or 9 ripe yellow peaches
3 tablespoons coconut
    sugar
2 tablespoons almond
    flour
⅛ teaspoon nutmeg
¼ teaspoon almond extract

topping
30 g/¼ cup almond flour
40 g/⅓ cup gluten-free
    oats
40 g/⅓ cup quinoa flour
3 tablespoons coconut
    sugar
¼ teaspoon nutmeg
60 g/½ cup sliced almonds
5 tablespoons melted
    coconut oil

an 23-cm/9-in pie dish,
    greased

serves 8

It's easy to take a seed and blend it into a tasty crust. Sunflower seeds work well in a sweet crust. I think the secret to flavouring a summer peach pie is almond extract, but be careful, as a little goes a long way!

Put dry ingredients in a food processor and pulse to a fine crumb. Add the melted coconut oil and pulse again until the mix is combined. Remove from the food processor and bind together in your hands to form a pastry. Wrap tightly in clingfilm/plastic wrap and chill in the refrigerator for 30 minutes.

Preheat the oven to 180ºC (350ºF) Gas 4.

Once chilled, press the crust evenly along the bottom of the prepared pie dish and up the sides. Poke holes in the pastry case with a fork. Then place the pastry case in the oven and bake for 20 minutes or until brown in colour. Do not turn off the oven.

For the filling, bring a pot of water to the boil over a high heat. Make a cross at the base of each peach. Then drop them one by one into the boiling water for 30 seconds. Remove then put in an ice water bath. This will allow you to easily peel off the skin of the peach. Once peeled, slice each peach into thin, even slices and place in a mixing bowl. Add the rest of the filling ingredients and mix.

Add the filling to the pre-cooked pastry case and set aside.

For the topping, mix all dry ingredients together in a large mixing bowl, then add the melted coconut oil. Mix together then, using your hands, crumble the topping all over the top of the pie, making sure you cover all of the peaches.

Bake the pie in the preheated oven for a further 35 minutes to cook the filling and topping. Leave to cool, then serve.

peanut butter quinoa cookies

420 g/1¾ cup creamy
  peanut butter
75 g/¾ cup xylitol or other
  sugar substitute
140 ml/¾ cup agave syrup
2 eggs (see Note)
1 teaspoon vanilla extract
45 g/½ cup quinoa flakes
2 tablespoons quinoa flour
½ teaspoon bicarbonate of
  soda/baking soda

*a baking sheet lined with
  parchment paper*

makes 24

These are good – really good. I get to use quinoa in its flake and flour form so, naturally, these cookies excite me. They never last for very long in my house.

Preheat the oven to 180ºC (350ºF) Gas 4.

Mix all ingredients together in a large mixing bowl. Once the ingredients are all combined, bring the mixture together in your hands then roll into 2½-cm/1-inch balls and place onto the prepared baking sheet. Using your thumb, press down each ball so it is slightly flattened out.

You can use your fingers for this which is great for getting children involved too.

Bake in the preheated oven for approximately 12 minutes, until the cookies are golden, and serve warm. Store the cookies in an airtight container for up to 3 days.

Note: If you prefer not to use eggs you could use egg replacer or make a flax-egg mix by combining 2 tablespoons of ground flaxseed with 6 tablespoons of water.

almond flour tea loaf with fresh berries

165 g/1½ cup almond
   flour
50 g/½ cup milled
   flaxseeds
1½ teaspoons baking
   powder
100 g/heaping 1 cup
   coconut sugar
125 g/½ cup melted
   coconut oil
1 teaspoon vanilla extract
4 eggs (see Note)
a handful of fresh berries,
   to serve
a dollop of clotted/thick
   cream, to serve

a 23 x 12½ cm/9 x 5 in loaf
   pan lined with baking
   parchment

serves 8

The greatest part of almond flour is that you don't need starches or binding agents to make delicious baked goods. Almonds are a superfood because they are rich in vitamins and minerals, and a good source of fat. This loaf can also be enjoyed as a breakfast treat.

Preheat the oven to 180°C (350°F) Gas 4.

Sift the almond flour into a large mixing bowl. Add in the other dry ingredients, then the melted oil and vanilla and mix together. Then add the eggs, and whisk using an electric whisk on high for 4 minutes until the batter gets becomes light and increases in volume.

Bake in the preheated oven for 40 minutes or until a knife comes out clean.

Garnish with fresh seasonal berries and serve with cream on the side.

Note: If you prefer not to use eggs you could use egg replacer or make a flax-egg mix by combining 2 tablespoons of ground flaxseed with 6 tablespoons of water.

index

acknowledgements

With love to my amazing mother Margery, the ultimate sous-chef.

Special thanks to my dearest husband Todd, and my son Jake, the ultimate taste testers, whose honesty was essential for this book. To the editors and team at Ryland Peters & Small for making such a beautiful book.

To some of my friends, family and colleagues who have supported me through the process. Margery Barr, Janet Ginns, Jason Barr, Susan Ginns, Helen Ginns, Gail and Richard Finegold, Lissa Purdy, Lindsey Haase, Jessica Minkoff, Brooke Jaffe, Lauren Brody, Taymour Hallal, Gail Lewenberg, Edward Sadovnik, Megan Turnas and the team at Whole Foods UK.